BISTRO

RYLAND
PETERS
& SMALL

LONDON NEW YORK

BISTRO

French country recipes for home cooks

Laura Washburn

Photography by Martin Brigdale

First published in the United States in 2003

This paperback edition published in 2008
by Ryland Peters & Small, Inc.
519 Broadway, 5th Floor
New York, NY 10012
www.rylandpeters.com

10 9 8 7 6 5 4 3 2 1

ISBN 978 1 84597 694 1

Printed and bound in China

Senior Designer Steve Painter
Commissioning Editor Elsa Petersen-Schepelern
Editor Susan Stuck
Production Meryl Silbert
Art Director Gabriella Le Grazie
Publishing Director Alison Starling

Food Stylist Linda Tubby
Stylist Helen Trent
Indexer Hilary Bird

Dedication

For Mom and John

Acknowledgments

Thank you to all who helped with the children,
especially Melissa Glase and Rachel Donovan, but
also Gail Ezra, Denise Clare, and Linda Daniels.
Thanks also to the Phillips family; Maha, Mike,
Lawrence, and Martha, who graciously gave up
many a Sunday to help with the eating and
critiquing. Wine and food matching advice came
from the experts at Apogée, Patrice and Erika
Marcoue, Le Puiset, France www.vinsapogee.com.
Thank you, Martin Brigdale, Linda Tubby, and
Helen Trent for making it look so beautiful, and
thanks to Steve Painter for enthusiasm and
helpful input, as well as great design. Thanks,
Ananda. And thanks, thanks, thanks to Julian,
Clara, and especially Jim.

Library of Congress Cataloging-in-Publication Data

Washburn, Laura.
  Bistro : French country recipes for home cooks /
Laura Washburn ;
photography by Martin Brigdale.
    p. cm.
  Originally published in the USA: 2003.
  Includes index.
  ISBN 978-1-84597-694-1
  1. Cookery, French. I. Title.
  TX719.W3397 2008
  641.5941--dc22
                                        2008003246

Notes

• All spoon measurements are level unless otherwise stated.

• Ovens should be preheated to the specified temperature. Recipes in this book were tested using a conventional oven. If using a fan oven, cooking times should be changed according to the manufacturer's instructions.

• For all recipes requiring dough or batter, liquid measurements are given as a guide. Always add liquid gradually to achieve the desired consistency, rather than adding it all at once. Use your eyes and your sense of touch to achieve the best results. If you don't use the flour specified in a recipe, the result may be affected.

contents

bistro is a way of life

People disagree about the origins of the word "bistro." Some say it was introduced by the Russians after the invasion of Paris in 1814, as they shouted "*bystro!*" (meaning "quickly!") at waiters in busy cafés. Some argue that it evolved from the Parisian slang of the time, and others trace the term to a northern dialect. But wherever the word began, the bistro experience has not strayed too far from its roots.

Restaurants and cafés sprang up all over France during the 19th century, primarily in Paris, but these upscale eating establishments were destined for the bourgeoisie. Bistros began at about the same time and the difference was in the clientele, the locality, and the atmosphere of the place. They were neighborhood watering holes, a sanctuary for the locals, a comforting, relaxed place for people to gather and socialize. Initially, bistros were as much about drinking as eating. Simple country wines were poured from carafes into chunky water glasses, while the regulars debated the political topics of the day. But this sort of activity requires sustenance and, gradually, bistros became like extensions of the home kitchen. So while "chefs" prepared elegant meals in the *grands restaurants*, cooks prepared modest food for the ordinary folks in local bistros.

Nowadays, the distinctions are blurred, and the terms "bistro" and "restaurant" are used almost interchangeably. Despite this, there does seem to be an implicit understanding that bistro is synonymous with simplicity. The reason is that bistro food is traditional, with roots in the regional specialities of France. For the most part, bistro menus often mimic the kind of meals prepared in homes. This is why authentic bistro fare is the essence of French cuisine. It is honest, fresh, and satisfying food prepared by cooks, not celebrity chefs. It uses local ingredients and seasonal produce. It is not expensive, it is not complicated, and it never goes out of fashion. Bistro food is real food, for real people.

There is nothing new about bistro. The recipes in this book are simply up-to-date versions of good, old-fashioned food. And despite all the conveniences of modern life, time is still short, so ingredients are basic, preparations are simple, and, for the health-conscious, butter and cream have been kept to a minimum. Suggestions for French regional wines to accompany many of the dishes have been provided because the best thing to drink with French food is French wine. It's also part of the fun, but feel free to substitute a local wine. Bistro food started in home kitchens, so there is no need for fancy equipment or great technical prowess. Better still, bistro is about making the most of ingredients; it's about value for money and it's about cooking with leftovers.

The stresses of life were surely different in the days when bistros began, but our need to escape, to relax, and to restore ourselves remains the same. Bistro food is like a trusted friend. It is reliable, it is comfortable, it is easy. It is what you want to come home to after a hard day's work. So the trends may come, and the trends will surely go, one thing that will remain constant is our appetite for authentic flavors and satisfying meals, which is why bistro cooking has enduring appeal.

But bistro is more than just a cuisine. It's a way of life. It's about taking the time to savor a meal and enjoy the company of family and friends. Bistro cooking is about bringing the pot straight to the table, dipping chunks of crusty baguette in a rich, simmered sauce, and washing it all down with French country wine. Bistro cuisine represents the best that France has to offer and the next best thing to being there (in France!) is to bring a bit of bistro to your own home. *Bon appétit!*

appetizers

This recipe is my version of a well-loved staple of Provençal cuisine. Purists will tell you that only Parisians add carrots and that aged Gouda is imperative. The reason, according to one story, is that this soup was invented by Italian workers building the railway in the hills above Nice, who used the Dutch cheese because there was a lot of it in transit at the port. A variation is to add peeled, seeded, and chopped tomatoes to the pistou.

soupe au pistou

3 tablespoons extra virgin olive oil

1 onion, chopped

1 small fennel bulb, quartered, cored, and chopped

2 zucchini, chopped

8 oz. new potatoes, chopped

2 vine-ripened tomatoes, peeled, seeded, and chopped

2 quarts vegetable or chicken stock, preferably organic*

a sprig of thyme

2 cups canned cannellini beans, 15.5 oz., drained

2 cups. canned red kidney beans, 15.5 oz., drained

6 oz. green beans, cut into 1-inch pieces, about 1 cup

1¾ oz. spaghetti, broken into pieces

5 oz. finely grated cheese (aged Gouda or Parmesan), about 1⅓ cups

coarse sea salt and freshly ground black pepper

Pistou

6 garlic cloves

a small bunch of basil, leaves only

⅓ cup extra virgin olive oil

Serves 4–6

Heat the oil in a large saucepan or casserole dish. Add the onion, fennel, and zucchini and cook over medium heat until browned, about 10 minutes. Add the potatoes, tomatoes, stock, and thyme. Bring to a boil, then cover and simmer gently for 15 minutes.

Add the drained cannellini and kidney beans and simmer, covered, for 15 minutes more. Taste and adjust the seasoning with salt and pepper. Add the green beans and the spaghetti and cook until the pasta is tender, about 10 minutes more. Cover and let stand. Ideally, the soup should rest for at least a few hours before serving, or make one day in advance and refrigerate. (Do not make the pistou until you are ready to serve; it is best fresh, and the basil and garlic should not be cooked.)

To make the pistou, put the garlic, basil, and oil in a small food processor and blend until well chopped. You can also make it using a mortar and pestle, starting with the garlic and finishing with the oil, added gradually. It is more authentic, but I've never been very good at this method.

To serve, heat the soup and pass round the pistou and cheese, to be stirred in to taste. The soup can also be served at room temperature.

*Note Unless your stock is homemade, it may contain salt, so season judiciously and taste the soup often as it cooks. Organic vegetable and organic chicken stocks are available in quart-size resealable boxes in supermarkets. There is no salt added, and the flavor is very good.

A classic case of less is more. This soup is soothing, restorative, and deliciously delicate, despite its rustic origins.

cabbage soup

soupe au chou

1½ lb. ham hock

1 onion, studded with a clove

1 fresh bay leaf

1 cabbage

1 inner celery stalk with leaves, cut into chunks

7 carrots, cut into chunks

4 turnips, cut into chunks

1 tablespoon unsalted butter, plus more for serving

1¾ lb. small new potatoes, peeled

coarse sea salt

Serves 4–6

Put the ham hock and onion in a large saucepan with 3 quarts water. Bring to a boil and skim off any foam that rises to the surface, then reduce the heat, cover, and let simmer.

Meanwhile, bring another saucepan of water to a boil with a bay leaf. When it boils, add the cabbage and blanch for 5 minutes. Remove the cabbage and drain. When cool enough to handle, slice the cabbage.

Add the sliced cabbage, celery, carrots, turnips, and butter to the pork. Taste for seasoning. Return to a boil, then lower the heat, cover, and simmer for about 30 minutes. Taste for seasoning again.

Add the potatoes and cook until they are tender, 20–25 minutes more. To serve, remove the ham hock and cut into bite-size pieces. Trim off any rind and discard any bones. Return the pieces to the soup and serve hot, with a spoonful of butter in each bowl and thick slices of country bread.

Variation

In France, cooks buy salt pork or ham hocks from the butcher. However if you would like to try, homemade salt pork is very simple to make; you will have to sacrifice some refrigerator space for three days, which is the only complication. But you will be well rewarded. You will need 1½ lb. spare ribs or similar cut and 6 tablespoons. pickling salt, which your butcher should be able to supply.

Three days before you plan to serve the soup, put the pork in a shallow ceramic or glass dish and add water to cover. Add the salt and stir until dissolved. Cover and refrigerate for 3 days, turning occasionally. Alternatively, have the butcher salt the pork for you.

The day of serving, remove the pork from its brine and rinse, then proceed as in the main recipe.

An old-fashioned nourishing soup, full of healthy green things. If you do not have sorrel growing in your garden (or available in your supermarket), it can be omitted.

kitchen garden soup

soupe du potager

1 fresh bay leaf

1 small cabbage, quartered

4 tablespoons unsalted butter

2 leeks, halved and sliced

1 onion, chopped

2 teaspoons salt

8 oz. new potatoes, chopped, about 1¼ cups

a handful of flat-leaf parsley, chopped

8 oz. freshly shelled peas, about 2 cups

1 romaine lettuce heart, quartered and sliced thinly

a bunch of sorrel, sliced

unsalted butter and/or sour cream or crème fraîche, to serve (optional)

sea salt and freshly ground black pepper

Serves 4–6

Put the bay leaf in a large saucepan of water and bring to a boil. Add the cabbage quarters and blanch for 3 minutes. Drain the cabbage, pat dry, and slice it thinly.

Heat the butter in a large saucepan. Add the cabbage, leeks, onion, and 2 teaspoons salt and cook until softened, 5–10 minutes. Add the potatoes, parsley, and 2 quarts water. Add salt and pepper to taste and simmer gently for 40 minutes.

Stir in the peas, lettuce, and sorrel and cook for 10 minutes more. Taste for seasoning. Ladle into bowls, add 1 tablespoon of butter and/or sour cream, if using, to each, and serve.

It is difficult to make true bouillabaisse outside France because so many of the fish used are found only in the Mediterranean. But here's a very good vegetable-only alternative, with all the same flavors, including the best part—the chile-spiked rouille sauce. Traditional versions include a poached egg, which I have omitted.

¼ cup extra virgin olive oil

2 leeks, white part only, halved lengthwise, then sliced crosswise

I large onion, coarsely chopped

I fennel bulb, halved, cored, and chopped

3 garlic cloves, crushed

3 large, vine-ripened tomatoes, peeled, seeded, and chopped

5 medium new potatoes, cubed

I teaspoon salt

2 quarts vegetable stock, preferably organic* or water

I fresh bay leaf

a sprig of thyme

a strip of peel from I unwaxed orange

I teaspoon good-quality saffron strands

I baguette loaf, sliced, for croutons

1½ cups freshly grated Gruyère cheese, about 5 oz.

coarse sea salt and freshly ground black pepper

a handful of chopped flat-leaf parsley, to serve

Rouille

3 garlic cloves, very finely chopped

1–2 red chiles, seeded and very finely chopped

I egg yolk, at room temperature

about 1¼ cups extra virgin olive oil

fine sea salt and freshly ground black pepper

a baking sheet

Serves 4–6

vegetable bouillabaisse
bouillabaisse borgne

Heat the oil in a large saucepan. Add the leeks, onions, and fennel and cook until just beginning to brown, about 10 minutes. Stir in the garlic, tomatoes, potatoes, and I teaspoon salt and cook for I minute. Add the stock or water, the bay leaf, thyme, orange peel, and saffron and stir. Bring to a boil, reduce the heat, and simmer gently until the potatoes are tender, about 40 minutes. Add salt and pepper to taste, cover, and let stand for at least I hour, or cool and refrigerate overnight.

Before you serve, make the croutons. Arrange the baguette slices in a single layer on a baking sheet. Bake in a preheated oven at 350°F until golden, about 5–8 minutes. Set aside.

To make the rouille, put the garlic, chiles, and egg yolk in a small, deep bowl. Beat well. Add the oil bit by bit and beating vigorously, until the mixture is thick like mayonnaise. Add fine salt and pepper to taste.

To serve, warm the soup if necessary. Put 2–3 croutons in each soup plate, sprinkle with the grated cheese, and ladle in the soup. Sprinkle with chopped parsley and serve with the rouille, to be stirred in according to taste.

*Note   Unless your stock is homemade, it may contain salt, so season judiciously and taste the soup often as it cooks. Organic vegetable and organic chicken stocks are available in quart-size resealable boxes in supermarkets. There is no salt added, and the flavor is very good.

Although this soup is synonymous with bistro eating, it is also associated with another tradition. At French weddings, especially in the countryside, it was often served in the early hours of the morning, as a restorative after a long night of celebrating. This recipe is a simplified version, the sort of thing that's ideal when it's chilly outside, people are hungry inside, and there's not much more than a few onions lurking about.

french onion soup
soupe gratinée à l'oignon

3 tablespoons unsalted butter

1 tablespoon extra virgin olive oil

3 large onions, about 3 lb., thinly sliced

2 garlic cloves, crushed

1 tablespoon all-purpose flour

1 quart beef or chicken stock, preferably organic

2¾ cups dry white wine

1 fresh bay leaf

2 sprigs of thyme

1 baguette, or other white bread, sliced

1½ cups freshly grated Gruyère cheese, about 5 oz.

coarse sea salt and freshly ground black pepper

a baking tray

Serves 4–6

Put the butter and oil in a large saucepan and melt over medium heat. Add the onions and cook over low heat until soft, 15–20 minutes.

Add the garlic and flour and cook, stirring, for about 1 minute. Add the stock, wine, bay leaf, and thyme. Season with salt and pepper and bring to a boil. Boil for 1 minute, then lower the heat and simmer very gently for 20 minutes. Taste and adjust the seasoning with salt and pepper. At this point, the soup will be cooked, but standing time will improve the flavor—at least 30 minutes.

Before serving, preheat the broiler. Put the baguette slices on a baking sheet and brown under the broiler until lightly toasted. Set aside.

To serve, ladle the soup into ovenproof bowls and top with a few toasted baguette rounds. Sprinkle grated cheese over the top and cook under the broiler until browned and bubbling. Serve immediately.

France has many fish soups but only this one includes hot chiles. Another plus is that it can be made successfully without hard-to-come-by Mediterranean fish and, if you use good-quality fresh fish stock, it's very quick to make. The bones and shrimp shells add flavor, as well as making it a bit messy, but this is fishermen's fare, so roll up your sleeves and enjoy.

basque fish soup

ttoro

2 tablespoons extra virgin olive oil

1 red bell pepper, halved, seeded, and sliced

1 onion, halved and sliced

3 garlic cloves, crushed

1 green chile, seeded and chopped

¼ teaspoon best-quality hot paprika

a sprig of thyme

1 cup canned chopped peeled tomatoes, 8 oz.

1½ quarts fresh fish stock

8 oz. monkfish fillet, cut into bite-size pieces

1 lb. hake or cod steaks

8 oz. unpeeled shrimp tails

1 cup dry white wine

1 lb. fresh mussels*

a handful of flat-leaf parsley, chopped

Croutons

1 baguette, sliced

2 garlic cloves, peeled

Serves 4–6

Heat the oil in a stockpot. Add the pepper and onion and cook until browned, about 5 minutes. Stir in the garlic, chile, paprika, thyme, and tomatoes and cook for 5 minutes more.

Add the fish stock, monkfish, hake, and shrimp. Bring to a boil, skim off the foam, and simmer gently until the fish is cooked through, 10–15 minutes.

Meanwhile, to make the croutons, arrange the baguette slices in a single layer on a baking sheet. Bake in a preheated oven at 350°F until golden, 5–8 minutes. Let cool slightly, then rub with garlic cloves and set aside.

Put the wine in a large saucepan with a lid and bring to a boil. Boil for 1 minute, then remove from the heat. Add the prepared mussels to the wine, cover, and steam over high heat just until opened, 2–3 minutes. Remove the mussels from their shells, discarding any that do not open.

Add the mussels and cooking liquid to the soup and stir well. Sprinkle with parsley and serve immediately, with the garlic croutons.

*Note To prepare mussels, start 15 minutes before you are ready to use. Rinse them in cold water and tap any open ones against the work surface. If they don't close, discard them. Scrub the others with a stiff brush and scrape off any barnacles. Pull off and discard the wiry beards.

Unlike most dishes cooked with cheese, this is very light and elegant, perfect to serve before a rich stew. It is also very moreish and you could be tempted to make a meal of it, at lunch perhaps, with a simple green salad. Alternatively, make individual tarts for a picnic, buffet or dinner party. Serve with a white wine from the Loire.

goat cheese tart
tarte au chèvre

1½ cups all-purpose flour, plus extra for rolling

7 tablespoons cold unsalted butter, cut into pieces

a pinch of salt

3–4 tablespoons cold water

Goat cheese filling

3 large eggs

1 cup sour cream or crème fraîche

3 Crottin de Chavignol goat cheeses, about 2–3 oz. each

2 oz. finely grated Gruyère cheese, about 1 cup

a small bunch of chives

fine sea salt

parchment paper and beans or baking weights

a loose-based tart pan, 11 inches diameter

Serves 4–6

To make the dough, put the flour, butter, and salt in a food processor and, using the pulse button, process until the butter is broken down (about 5–10 pulses). Add 3 tablespoons cold water and pulse just until the mixture forms coarse crumbs; add 1 more tablespoon if necessary, but do not do more than 10 pulses.

Transfer the dough to a sheet of parchment paper, form into a ball, and flatten to a disk. Wrap in the paper and refrigerate for 30–60 minutes.

Roll out the dough on a floured work surface to a disk slightly larger than the tart pan. Carefully transfer the dough to the pan, patching any holes as you go, and pressing gently into the sides. To trim the edges, roll a rolling pin over the top, using the edge of the pan as a cutting surface, and letting the excess fall away. Tidy up the edges and refrigerate until firm, about 30–60 minutes.

Prick the dough all over, line with the parchment paper, and fill with beans or weights. Bake in a preheated oven at 400°F for 15 minutes, then remove the paper and weights and bake until just golden, 10–15 minutes more. Let the tart crust cool slightly before filling. Do not turn off the oven

To make the filling, put the eggs, sour cream, and a large pinch of salt in a bowl and beat well. Slice each goat cheese into 3 rounds and arrange in the tart crust. Pour in the egg mixture and sprinkle with the Gruyère. Snip the chives with kitchen shears and sprinkle over the top. Bake for 20–30 minutes or until browned. Serve warm.

Green salads do not appear as often on French menus as an appetizer or side dish as they do in other countries, though they are still served in very traditional bistros. Home is the main place for eating salads, and they're eaten daily, usually after the entrée and either before or with the cheese. Raw garlic is not always included, but the vinaigrette method is classic, the way I was taught to make it when I first moved to France, and the way I've made it ever since.

mixed greens with garlic vinaigrette
salade verte, vinaigrette à l'ail

2 tablespoons wine vinegar

½ teaspoon fine sea salt

I teaspoon Dijon mustard

⅓ cup extra virgin olive oil

2 garlic cloves, crushed

freshly ground pepper

8 oz. tender, mixed salad greens, washed and dried

a handful of flat-leaf parsley, coarsely chopped

a small bunch of chives, snipped with kitchen shears

Serves 4

Put the vinegar in your salad bowl. Using a fork or a small whisk, beat in the salt until almost dissolved. You may have to tilt the bowl so the vinegar is deep enough to have something to stir. Mix in the mustard until completely blended. Add the oil, a tablespoon at a time, beating well between each addition, until emulsified. Mix in the garlic and pepper to taste.

If you like a powerful garlic punch, tear the lettuce into smallish pieces, add to the bowl with the parsley and chives, then toss. Serve immediately. I prefer to let the garlic sit in the dressing for at least 30 minutes to mellow it a bit. In any case, do not add the lettuce until you are ready to serve or it will be soggy.

Anchoïade is a Provençal anchovy sauce/dip, which is spread thickly on grilled bread slices, or served with raw vegetables as an appetizer. Here it becomes a dressing for what will hopefully be very ripe, flavorful tomatoes. If these are not available, use boiled baby new potatoes instead and toss while the potatoes are still warm. Serve with a chilled Provençal rosé and lots of crusty bread.

1½ lb. vine-ripened tomatoes

1 large shallot, or 1 small red onion, thinly sliced

coarse sea salt and freshly ground black pepper

Anchovy vinaigrette

1 garlic clove

½ teaspoon Dijon mustard

2 tablespoons white wine vinegar

6 anchovy fillets, packed in oil

½ cup extra virgin olive oil

a small handful of basil leaves

freshly ground black pepper

To serve

a handful of flat-leaf parsley, finely chopped

a few basil leaves, torn

Serves 4

tomato salad with anchovy vinaigrette

salade de tomates, vinaigrette à l'anchoïade

To make the vinaigrette, put the garlic, mustard, vinegar, and anchovies in a small food processor and blend well. Add the oil, 1 tablespoon at a time, then blend in the basil. Season with pepper and set aside.

Cut the tomatoes into quarters or eighths, depending on their size. Arrange on a plate and sprinkle with the shallot. Season lightly with salt, then spoon the dressing over the top. Sprinkle with the parsley, basil, and freshly ground black pepper, and serve at room temperature.

belgian endive salad
with roquefort, celery, and walnuts

salade d'endives aux roquefort, céleri et noix

4–5 heads of Belgian endive, about 1¼ lb., halved, cored, and thinly sliced

2 celery stalks, thinly sliced, plus a few leaves, torn

3 oz. Roquefort cheese, crumbled, about 1 cup

⅓ cup shelled walnuts, chopped, about 2 oz.

a handful of flat-leaf parsley, finely chopped

1 baguette, sliced, to serve

Walnut vinaigrette

2 tablespoons wine vinegar

1 teaspoon fine sea salt

1 teaspoon Dijon mustard

7 tablespoons safflower oil (see method)

1 tablespoon walnut oil (optional)

freshly ground pepper

Serves 4

Mine is a family of serial salad eaters, but I'd never heard of—let alone tasted—Belgian endive until moving to France. In those days, it was still a fairly bitter thing, available only in winter and an acquired taste, but it has come a long way. Developed unintentionally by a gardener at the Brussels botanical gardens in the middle of the nineteenth century, Belgian endive is now cultivated for a good part of the year, and modern varieties have none of the bitterness of their ancestors. When buying, choose very pale endives with only a hint of green; they grow in the dark, so color on the leaves is a sign that they have been exposed to the light and are not as fresh. Also, big is not necessarily better; 8 inches is the maximum length for best taste.

To prepare the vinaigrette, put the vinegar in the bowl you plan to serve in. Using a fork or a small whisk, beat in the salt until almost dissolved. You may have to tilt the bowl so the vinegar is deep enough to have something to stir. Mix in the mustard until completely blended. Add the oil, a tablespoon at a time, beating well between each addition, until emulsified. If you're using the walnut oil, use one less tablespoon of safflower oil. Stir in pepper to taste.

Just before you're ready to serve the salad, add the endive, celery, Roquefort, walnuts, and parsley and toss well. Serve immediately, with sliced baguette.

Before school holidays imposed August-only restrictions on our travel, we always went to Cassis in September. We loved to picnic in the middle *calanque*—swimming, sunning, and, of course, eating. For the occasion, I would buy this salad from a tiny butcher's shop in the back lanes. It was made by an Algerian, which explains the cumin and makes all the difference.

chickpea salad
salade de pois chiches

1½ cups dried chickpeas, about 8 oz.

1 fresh bay leaf

2 red bell peppers, halved, seeded, and sliced

2 tablespoons extra virgin olive oil

1 teaspoon herbes de provence

1 large shallot, chopped

a large handful of flat-leaf parsley, chopped

coarse sea salt and freshly ground black pepper

Vinaigrette

2 teaspoons cumin seeds

3 tablespoons wine vinegar

1 teaspoon fine sea salt

10 tablespoons extra virgin olive oil

freshly ground black pepper

Serves 4–6

One day before serving, soak the chickpeas in cold water to cover, and put in the refrigerator. Next day, drain the chickpeas. Transfer to a saucepan and cover with cold water. Add the bay leaf and bring to a boil. When the water boils, lower the heat, cover, and simmer until tender, about 2 hours. Check occasionally and add more water if necessary. Add 1 teaspoon coarse sea salt 30 minutes before the end of cooking time.

Meanwhile, put the bell peppers in a small baking dish, toss with the oil, herbs, and 1 teaspoon salt. Roast in a preheated oven at 425°F until beginning to char, 20–25 minutes. Remove from the oven. When cool, cut into dice and set aside.

To make the vinaigrette, sauté the cumin seeds in a hot, dry skillet until they begin to pop and you can smell their aroma. Immediately crush them to a powder with a mortar and pestle.

Put the vinegar in a small bowl. Using a fork or a small whisk, beat in the fine sea salt until almost dissolved. You may have to tilt the bowl so the vinegar is deep enough to have something to stir. Add the oil, a tablespoon at a time, beating well between each addition, until emulsified. Mix in the cumin and pepper to taste.

When the chickpeas are cooked, drain thoroughly and transfer to a serving bowl; a wide, shallow one is best, to ensure a maximum of dressing comes into contact with the chickpeas. Add the vinaigrette, red pepper, and shallot. Toss well and add salt and pepper to taste. Add the parsley, toss again, and serve warm or at room temperature.

Crudités are a classic appetizer, especially in Parisian cafés and bistros, and they are a favorite of mine. The combination of vegetables given is fairly representative, but it does vary. Canned corn and tuna are common, as are hard-cooked eggs. You could quite easily make a meal of this by increasing the quantities or adding other ingredients to make it more elegant and contemporary. Try blanched asparagus tips, sliced cherry tomatoes, peeled blanched fava beans, or wafer-thin red onion slices.

crudités

2 tablespoons wine vinegar

¼ red cabbage, thinly sliced

8 oz. baby new potatoes

4 oz. baby green beans, topped and tailed

3 medium carrots, grated

1 tablespoon freshly squeezed lemon juice

3 cooked beets

1 medium cucumber

a handful of flat-leaf parsley, finely chopped

fine sea salt

1 baguette, sliced, to serve

Vinaigrette

3 tablespoons wine vinegar

1 teaspoon fine sea salt

2 teaspoons Dijon mustard

11 tablespoons safflower oil

freshly ground black pepper

Serves 4

To make the vinaigrette, put the vinegar in a bowl. Using a fork or a small whisk, beat in the salt until almost dissolved. You may have to tilt the bowl so the vinegar is deep enough to have something to stir. Mix in the mustard until completely blended. Add the oil, 1 tablespoon at a time, beating well between each addition, until emulsified. Add pepper to taste. Set aside.

Heat the 2 tablespoons vinegar in a wok. As soon as it boils, remove from the heat, add the red cabbage, and toss well. Salt lightly and set aside until the cabbage turns an even, deep, fuchsia color.

Meanwhile, put the potatoes in a saucepan with cold water to cover. Bring to a boil, add salt, and cook until tender, about 15 minutes. Drain, peel, and slice thinly.

Bring another saucepan of water to a boil, add salt, then the beans. Cook until just tender, 3–5 minutes. Drain and set aside.

Put the carrots, lemon juice, and a pinch of salt in a bowl and toss well; set aside. Cut the beets in quarters lengthwise, then slice thinly to get small triangular pieces. Peel the cucumber (if you like), cut it in quarters lengthwise, and slice.

Arrange small mounds of each ingredient on plates, alternating colors. Add a few spoonfuls of vinaigrette to each one and sprinkle with parsley. Serve with a basket of sliced baguette.

Light, lovely leeks in a lively, herb-studded sauce. Serve these at the start of a substantial spread, to allow room for expansion, or as part of a light lunch, with the Goat Cheese Tart on page 22. If you can't find sorrel, it will be a shame, but the recipe works without, so don't feel obliged to replace it with anything.

baby leeks with herb vinaigrette
poireaux, vinaigrette aux herbes

1½ lb. baby leeks
¼ cup wine vinegar
1 teaspoon Dijon mustard
1 teaspoon fine sea salt
1 cup safflower oil
a small handful of flat-leaf parsley
a small handful of watercress
a small handful of tarragon
3 sorrel leaves
freshly ground black pepper
2 shallots, thinly sliced
a small bunch of chives, snipped with kitchen shears

Serves 4

Put the leeks in the top of a steamer and cook until tender, about 7–10 minutes. Remove and set aside to drain.

To make the vinaigrette, put the vinegar, mustard, and salt in a small food processor and blend well. Add about ⅓ cup of the oil and blend for a few seconds. Continue adding the oil, bit by bit, and blending until the vinaigrette is emulsified. Add the parsley, watercress, tarragon, and sorrel and pulse again to chop. Add pepper to taste. (Alternatively, see page 25 for the hand-mixing method, and you should chop all the herbs finely.)

If the leeks are still too wet, pat dry with paper towels. Arrange the leeks in a serving dish, spoon the vinaigrette over the top, and sprinkle with shallot slices and chives. Serve with any remaining vinaigrette on the side.

mackerel pâté

rillettes de maquereaux

2 mackerel, about 14 oz. each, well cleaned, with heads on

1 onion, sliced

3 tablespoons unsalted butter, cut into pieces and melted or softened

a large handful of flat-leaf parsley

a few sprigs of tarragon, leaves stripped

freshly squeezed juice of 1 lemon

a dash of Tabasco

coarse sea salt and freshly ground black pepper

Court bouillon

1 carrot, sliced

1 onion, sliced

1 organic lemon, sliced

a sprig of thyme

1 fresh bay leaf

a few black peppercorns

1 clove

1 bottle dry white wine, 750 ml

2 teaspoons salt

To serve

toast or baguette

lemon wedges

Serves 6–8

Rillettes—a coarse but spreadable pâté—is normally made from pork or goose. This is a lighter version, made from mackerel poached in white wine, giving it a pleasant, almost pickled taste. Serve this straight from the bowl, passing it around the table at the start of an informal gathering, or spread it on crackers and serve with drinks. There's no point making this in small batches—but it freezes well, in case this is more than you need, or if you have leftovers.

One day before serving, put all the court bouillon ingredients in a saucepan. Bring to a boil over high heat, boil for 1 minute, then cover and simmer gently for 20 minutes.

Make 3 slits in the mackerels on either side, to help the flavors to penetrate the flesh. Put in a large baking dish and pour over the hot court bouillon. Cook in a preheated oven at 300°F for 30 minutes. Let cool in the liquid, then cover and refrigerate overnight.

The day of serving, remove the mackerel from the dish and lift the fillets, removing as many bones as possible.

Put the fillets, and most of the onion, in a food processor. Add the butter, parsley, and tarragon and blend briefly. Transfer to a serving bowl and stir in the lemon juice, Tabasco, and a generous grinding of pepper. Taste and adjust the seasoning.

Refrigerate until firm, then serve with toast or sliced baguette.

rustic pâté with green peppercorns
terrine de campagne au poivre vert

1 lb. boneless pork shoulder (fat *not* trimmed), ground

1 lb. veal, ground

8 oz. calves' liver, finely chopped

1 large egg, beaten

2 shallots, finely chopped

2 garlic cloves, crushed

1 tablespoon coarse sea salt

freshly ground black pepper

2 tablespoons green peppercorns in brine, drained, plus extra for decorating

½ teaspoon ground allspice

3 tablespoons Cognac

a handful of fresh bay leaves (see method)

To serve

French cornichons

unsalted butter

sliced baguette

a rectangular terrine mold, 12 x 4 inches

parchment paper

Serves 10–12

If you've never made your own terrine, try this. It is simplicity itself, and you may never get store-bought pâtés again. If you ask your butcher to grind all the meat, except the liver, then it will be even easier. Serve in slices to begin an informal meal, with plenty of fresh baguette, unsalted butter, and French cornichons. It also makes a great sandwich filling.

Put the pork, veal, and liver in a large bowl. Add the egg, shallots, garlic, salt, pepper, green peppercorns, allspice, and Cognac and mix well, preferably with your hands.

Fill the mold with the meat mixture, patting to spread evenly. Arrange bay leaves on top of the mold and dot with extra green peppercorns. Set it in a roasting pan and add enough boiling water to come halfway up the sides of the mold. Cover the terrine with foil and bake in a preheated oven at 350°F until a knife inserted in the middle is hot to the touch after 30 seconds, about 1½ hours.

Remove from the oven and let cool. When the terrine is at room temperature, cover with parchment paper and weight with a few food cans. Refrigerate, with the weights on top. Leave for at least 1 day, but 3 days is best. The pâté will keep, refrigerated, for 1 week. Bring to room temperature before serving.

entrées

I am utterly addicted to this dish with its buttery-lemony sauce. Sole is a well-crafted fish, both meaty and delicate at the same time, and is very easy to eat, bone-wise. Do not make this for a crowd, because you should eat it straight away and two soles are about all that will fit into the average nonstick skillet. But it is ideal for a tête-à-tête, weekday or otherwise, when you need something elegant and satisfying, in no time at all. Serve with a dry French white, a Chablis for example.

sole meunière

all-purpose flour
2 soles, about 10 oz. skinned and cleaned
4 tablespoons unsalted butter
2 tablespoons safflower oil
fine sea salt
freshly squeezed juice of ½ lemon

To serve
a handful of flat-leaf parsley, finely chopped
½ lemon, thinly sliced

Serves 2

Put some flour on a large plate, add the fish, cover with flour on both sides, and shake off the excess.

Reserve 2 tablespoons of the butter. Heat the oil and remaining butter over medium-high heat in a nonstick skillet large enough to hold both fish side by side. When it sizzles, add the sole and cook for 3 minutes. Turn them over and cook on the other side for about 3 minutes. Sprinkle the first side with salt while the second side is cooking.

When the fish is cooked through, transfer to warmed dinner plates and season the second side.

Return the skillet to the heat, add the reserved 2 tablespoons butter and melt over high heat. When it begins to sizzle, lower the heat and add the lemon juice. Cook, scraping the pan for about 10 seconds; do not let the butter burn. Pour this sauce over the fish and sprinkle with parsley. Serve immediately with sliced lemon.

Roughly translated, the English version of this dish means "roast from the sea." A gigot is the leg, usually of lamb, but here it refers to the sturdy, meaty nature of monkfish. Most other fish would be overwhelmed by the robust flavors in this Provençal preparation. There is certainly nothing fishy about this, which makes it ideal for those who are less than enthusiastic about eating food from the sea. Good fishmongers will make sure the thin grey membrane that lies under the skin is removed; but if it isn't, insist that it is, all the way down the tail, because it's a difficult job to do at home.

whole roast monkfish
gigot de mer

1 monkfish tail, about 18 oz.

about 12 thin slices bacon or prosciutto—enough to cover the fish

2 tablespoons extra virgin olive oil

1½ cups sliced mushrooms, about 8 oz.

2 large garlic cloves, crushed

1 cup dry white wine

2 lb. vine-ripened tomatoes, peeled, seeded, and chopped

2 tablespoons sour cream or crème fraîche

a handful of basil leaves, chopped

coarse sea salt and freshly ground black pepper

Serves 4

Preheat the oven to 425°F. Set the bacon on a work surface with the slices slightly overlapping each other. Put the monkfish on top, belly up. Wrap it in the bacon with the ends overlapping across the belly. Turn it over and set aside.

Heat the oil in a large skillet. Add the mushrooms and a pinch of salt and cook until browned, 3–5 minutes. Stir in the garlic, then add the wine, and cook over high heat for 1 minute. Stir in the tomatoes, salt lightly, and simmer gently for 5 minutes.

Pour this tomato sauce into a baking dish just large enough to hold the fish. Set the fish on top and roast for 15 minutes. Lower the temperature to 400°F and roast for 30 minutes more. Remove from the oven and put the fish on a plate. Stir the sour cream and basil into the tomatoes. Set the monkfish back on top and serve.

braised sea bass and fennel with saffron and harissa

bar braisé au fenouil epicé

Sea bass and fennel are virtually inseparable in Provençal cuisine. The market fish stalls of the south always have a plentiful supply of gleaming silvery bass, while fennel grows wild all over the countryside, so it's no wonder. Saffron and harissa, a spicy Tunisian chile paste, are not traditional, but recipes and ingredients from the former French colonies in North Africa are now found all over France, especially in the south. Serve with a Bandol rosé.

3 tablespoons extra virgin olive oil

1 onion, thinly sliced

3 large fennel bulbs, quartered and thinly sliced

2 cups fresh fish stock

a large pinch of saffron threads

2 small sea bass, cleaned and heads removed if preferred

8 oz. red potatoes, peeled and boiled

1–2 teaspoons harissa paste

coarse sea salt

Serves 2

Heat the oil in a large sauté pan with a lid. Add the onion and fennel and cook until lightly golden brown, about 5 minutes. Season lightly with salt.

Add the fish stock and saffron, cover, and simmer gently for 15 minutes.

Season the fish inside and out. Put the fish on top of the fennel, cover, and simmer gently until the fish is cooked through, 10–15 minutes.

Meanwhile, coarsely crush the potatoes with a fork and set aside.

Remove the fish, set them on large dinner plates, and keep them warm in a low oven. Raise the heat and cook the fennel mixture over high heat for 5 minutes. Add the crushed potatoes and harissa and continue cooking, covered, until warmed through, about 5 minutes more. Taste and adjust the seasoning with salt and pepper, spoon onto the plates beside the fish, and serve.

Variation Replace the crushed potatoes with couscous, but serve alongside the fish and vegetables instead of mixing it in; stir the harissa into the fennel before serving. For the couscous, follow the package instructions for serving size and cooking time.

A traditional dish from the Basque region, where tuna abounds and chiles are appreciated more than in other parts of France. This is quick to prepare and doesn't require long simmering, perfect when you want something hearty and full of flavor in about an hour.

⅓ cup extra virgin olive oil

2 onions, sliced

3 green bell peppers, halved, seeded, and sliced

3 red bell peppers, halved, seeded, and sliced

1½ lb. red tuna steaks, cut into 2-inch pieces

3 large, hot green chiles, seeded and sliced

4 vine-ripened tomatoes, peeled, seeded, and chopped

4 garlic cloves, crushed

2 lb. medium new potatoes, peeled and sliced into wedges

1 bottle dry white wine

coarse sea salt and freshly ground black pepper

Serves 4

tuna stew with chiles and potatoes
thon marmitako

Heat the oil in a large casserole dish. Add the onions and peppers and cook over high heat until brown, 3–5 minutes. Remove from the pan to a bowl and season with salt and pepper. Add the tuna and chiles to the pan, and cook to sear, 3–5 minutes. Add the tomatoes, garlic, and potatoes, then add salt to taste and stir carefully.

Return the onion mixture to the pan and pour in the wine. Add 1 cup water. Bring to a boil and boil for 1 minute, then reduce the heat, cover, and simmer gently until the potatoes are cooked through, 30–35 minutes. Serve immediately.

Salt cod and snails are traditional ingredients in this Provençal dish, but salmon and shrimp are easier to come by for most people. Be sure to use very good oil; despite great quantities of garlic, the flavor base of the aïoli comes from the oil, so it is worth investing in something special. Serve for a crowd, with everything freshly cooked and warmish, or at room temperature. Wash it all down with a chilled white or rosé from Provence.

le grand aïoli

¼ cup extra virgin olive oil

4 salmon steaks

8 oz. unpeeled shrimp tails

10 oz. small new potatoes

12 oz. asparagus tips

8 oz. small green beans

1 fresh bay leaf

6 baby carrots, sliced lengthwise

1 cauliflower, broken into florets

1 broccoli, broken into florets

8 oz. baby zucchini, halved lengthwise

6 eggs

6 oz. cherry tomatoes

4 cooked beets

coarse sea salt

Aïoli

2 egg yolks

about 1⅓ cups best-quality extra virgin olive oil

6 large garlic cloves

fine sea salt

Serves 6

Heat 1 tablespoon of the oil in a large nonstick skillet, add the salmon, and cook for about 3 minutes on each side, or until just cooked through. Season with salt and set aside. Add another 1 tablespoon of the oil to the pan. When hot, add the shrimp and cook until pink and firm, 3–5 minutes. Do not overcook or they will be tough. Season and set aside.

Put the potatoes in a saucepan with cold water to cover and bring to a boil. When the water boils, add salt and cook until tender, 15–20 minutes. Drain and set aside. Meanwhile, cook the asparagus tips and beans in boiling salted water until just tender, about 3 minutes.

Bring a saucepan of water to a boil with the bay leaf. When it boils, add the carrots and cook until al dente, 3–4 minutes. Remove with a slotted spoon and set aside. Return the water to a boil, add the cauliflower florets, and cook until just tender, about 5 minutes. Remove with a slotted spoon. Return the water to a boil, add the broccoli, and cook until just tender, 3–4 minutes.

Rub the zucchini all over with the remaining oil. Heat a ridged stovetop grill pan. When hot, add the zucchini pieces and cook, about 4 minutes per side. Alternatively, cook the same way in a nonstick skillet. Remove and season.

Put the eggs in a saucepan with cold water to cover. Bring to a boil and cook for 6 minutes from boiling point. Drain, cool under running water, then peel and slice.

To make the aïoli, put the egg yolks in a small, deep bowl. Beat well, then gradually beat in the oil, adding it bit by bit and beating vigorously, until the mixture is as thick as mayonnaise. Stir in the garlic and season to taste.

Arrange all the vegetables and fish on a single platter, or on several platters. Serve, passing the aïoli separately.

Large bowls of steaming hot mussels are served in bistros all over France. The classic recipe is *à la marinière*, with shallots and white wine. My combination of ingredients evolved because I could eat mussels every day, just steamed plain, but my husband does not share this enthusiasm. If, however, they come in a garlicky, saffron-scented sauce, reminiscent of summer holidays, then everyone is happy.

mussels with fennel, tomatoes, garlic and saffron
moules à la bouillabaisse

2 tablespoons extra virgin olive oil

1 small onion, chopped

½ fennel bulb, chopped

4 garlic cloves, crushed

1 cup dry white wine

2 cups canned chopped peeled tomatoes, 16 oz.

a pinch of saffron threads

2 lb. fresh mussels

coarse sea salt and freshly ground black pepper

a handful of flat-leaf parsley, chopped, to serve

Serves 4

Heat the oil in a large sauté pan. Add the onion and fennel and cook until soft, 3–5 minutes. Add the garlic, wine, and tomatoes. Boil for 1 minute, then lower the heat, then add the saffron and a pinch of salt. Simmer gently for 15 minutes.

Just before serving, clean and debeard the mussels, discarding any that do not close. (To prepare mussels, see note on page 21.)

Raise the heat under the sauce and, when boiling, add the prepared mussels. Cover and cook until the mussels open, 2–3 minutes. Discard any that do not open. Serve immediately, sprinkled with parsley.

Variation French fries are the classic accompaniments for mussels when served as a entrée. See the recipe on page 79.

On a recent visit to France, we went to the elegant seaside town of Hossegor. We window-shopped around the center, then strolled through the back streets, trying to choose which villa we would buy when we won the lottery. By the time we got to the seafront, we were famished. The first restaurant we saw had *chipirons à l'ail* written on the blackboard so we sat down, ordered some, and had a most memorable meal. *Chipirons* are tiny squid, very sweet and delicate, and unavailable where I live, but shrimp are a good substitute. Serve with lots of bread to mop up the garlicky sauce.

garlic shrimp
crevettes à l'ail

½ cup olive oil

2 lb. shrimp tails, with shells

8–10 garlic cloves, chopped

a large handful of flat-leaf parsley, chopped

coarse sea salt and freshly ground black pepper

1 lemon, cut into wedges, to serve

Serves 4

Heat the oil in a large sauté pan. When hot but not smoking, add the shrimp and garlic and cook until the shrimp turn pink, 3–5 minutes. Be careful not to let the garlic burn. Remove from the heat, sprinkle with salt, freshly ground black pepper, and parsley and mix well. Serve immediately, with lemon wedges.

This poor man's version of a dish in which truffle slices are stuffed under the chicken skin makes a nice change from ordinary roast chicken. The perfume of bay leaves and thyme delicately flavors the chicken flesh, while the tartness of the lemon keeps it lively.

roast chicken with bay leaves, thyme, and lemon
poulet rôti aux herbes et citron

1 free-range chicken, preferably organic, about 3 lb.

2 unwaxed lemons, preferably organic, 1 quartered, 1 sliced

6 large fresh bay leaves

2 sprigs of thyme

1–2 tablespoons extra virgin olive oil or 2 tablespoons butter

1 teaspoon dried thyme

1 onion, sliced in rounds

1 cup dry white wine (optional)

1 tablespoon unsalted butter

coarse sea salt

a roasting pan with a rack

Serves 4

Season the inside of the chicken generously and stuff with the lemon quarters, 2 of the bay leaves, and the thyme.

Using your fingers, separate the skin from the breast meat to create a little pocket and put 1 bay leaf on each side of the breast, underneath the skin. Put the remaining 2 bay leaves under the skin of the thighs. Rub the outside of the chicken all over with oil or butter, season generously, and sprinkle all over with the dried thyme.

Put the chicken on its side on a rack set over a roasting pan. Add water to fill the bottom of the pan by about ½ inch and add the sliced lemon and onion. Cook in a preheated oven at 425°F for 40 minutes, then turn the chicken on its other side. Continue roasting the chicken until cooked through and the juices run clear when a thigh is pierced with a skewer, about 40 minutes more. Add more water to the pan if necessary during cooking.

Remove from the oven, remove the chicken from the rack to a plate, and let stand, covered, for 10 minutes. Add 1 cup water, or the wine if using, to the pan juices and cook over high heat, scraping the bottom of the pan, 3–5 minutes. Stir in the butter. Carve the chicken and serve with the pan juices.

chicken with peppers, onions, ham, and tomatoes
poulet basquaise

2 tablespoons extra virgin olive oil

1 free-range chicken, about 4 lb., cut into 8 pieces

2 onions, sliced

2 red bell peppers, halved, seeded, and sliced

2 yellow bell peppers, halved, seeded, and sliced

2–4 large garlic cloves, crushed

2 small hot green chiles, seeded and thinly sliced (or ½ teaspoon hot red pepper flakes)

1 thick slice jambon de Bayonne or other unsmoked ham, about 1 inch thick and 6 oz., cut into strips

2 lb. vine-ripened tomatoes, peeled, seeded, and chopped

coarse sea salt and freshly ground black pepper

Serves 4

Like all traditional dishes, there are many versions of this recipe; some call only for green peppers, some use only onions and chiles. I think chiles are imperative, and if you want to be completely authentic, use *piment d'Espelette*, which is a most delicious little chile grown in the Basque region of France, but very difficult to find outside this area. They are pleasantly spicy without being overpowering, so whatever chile you use, resist the temptation to overdo it. Serve with rice.

Heat the oil in a large sauté pan with a lid, add the chicken pieces skin side down, and cook until brown, 5–10 minutes. Don't crowd the pan; if you can't fit all the pieces at once, brown in batches. Transfer the chicken to a plate, season well with salt, and set aside.

Add the onions and peppers to the pan, season with salt and black pepper, then cook over medium heat until soft, 15–20 minutes. Stir in the garlic, chiles, and ham and cook for 1 minute. Add the tomatoes, mix well, then add all the chicken pieces and bury them under the sauce. Cover and cook over low heat until the chicken is tender, 30–40 minutes. Taste for seasoning after 20 minutes. This dish can be made in advance and even improves after a night in the refrigerator.

Poulet sauté is at home all over France, but I especially like this southeastern version with its assertive flavors. It goes well with rice or fresh pasta such as the saffron tagliatelle used here, and a sturdy red wine, from the sun-baked south. Try a Collioure or a Minervois.

chicken with tomatoes, garlic, and olives
poulet sauté niçoise

2 tablespoons extra virgin olive oil

1 free-range chicken, about 4 lb., cut into 6–8 pieces

8 garlic cloves, finely chopped

2 cups canned chopped peeled tomatoes, 16 oz.

a pinch of sugar

2 oz. black olives, preferably niçoise, pitted and coarsely chopped, about ⅓ cup

coarse sea salt and freshly ground black pepper

a bunch of fresh basil, torn

Serves 4–6

Heat 1 tablespoon of the oil in a large sauté pan. Add the chicken pieces and brown on all sides. Transfer the chicken to a plate, salt generously, and set aside. Add the remaining oil and garlic and cook for 1 minute; do not let it burn. Add the tomatoes and sugar. Stir well and return the chicken pieces to the pan. Cover and simmer gently until the chicken is cooked, 25–30 minutes.

Transfer the chicken pieces to a serving dish, then raise the heat and cook the sauce to thicken slightly, about 10 minutes. Add salt and pepper to taste, then stir in the olives. Pour the sauce over the chicken pieces, sprinkle with the basil, and serve immediately.

A dish without a region, this is served pretty much all over France, in homes as well as restaurants. It's quick to make, if you get your butcher to cut up the chicken, and the flavor of tarragon lifts this out of the ordinary. Make this dish midweek and you'll have a lovely supper on the table in under an hour, or serve it for your next dinner party and it will seem like you slaved away all day. A red St-Estèphe or Ladoix would be the ideal wine.

chicken with tarragon
poulet sauté à l'estragon

1 tablespoon unsalted butter

1 tablespoon safflower oil

1 free-range chicken, about 4 lb., cut into 6–8 pieces

2 carrots, chopped

1 shallot or ½ small onion, chopped

a sprig of thyme

2–3 sprigs of flat-leaf parsley

a bunch of tarragon

3 tablespoons sour cream or crème fraîche

coarse sea salt and freshly ground black pepper

Serves 4

Melt the butter and oil in a large sauté pan with a lid. Add the chicken pieces and cook until brown, about 5 minutes. Work in batches if your pan is not big enough. Put the browned chicken pieces on a plate and season well with salt and pepper.

Add the carrots and shallot and cook, stirring for a minute or so. Return the chicken to the pan and add water to cover halfway. Add the thyme, parsley, and a few sprigs of tarragon. Cover and simmer gently for 30 minutes.

Meanwhile, strip the leaves from the remaining tarragon, chop them finely, and set aside. Add the stems to the cooking chicken.

Remove the chicken from the pan and put in a serving dish. Remove and discard the tarragon stems. (The recipe can be prepared a few hours in advance up to this point, then completed just before serving.)

Raise the heat and cook the sauce until reduced by half. Strain and return the sauce to the pan. Stir in the sour cream and the chopped tarragon. Heat briefly (do not boil) and pour over the chicken. Serve immediately.

If you can find a true guinea fowl, from a butcher or specialist supplier, then this will taste as it should (see Mail Order and Websites, page 142). It is worth the effort to search out the real thing because supermarket guinea fowl is disappointing, to say the least. The flavor bears no resemblance to anything worth paying money for; you are better off buying an organic or free-range chicken, since the preparation is the same and the result will be superior. Fortunately, the lentils will never disappoint.

guinea fowl with lentils
pintade aux lentilles

1 guinea fowl, about 3 lb.

3 tablespoons extra virgin olive oil

1 cup dried green lentils, preferably French

a sprig of thyme

1 fresh bay leaf

4 large shallots, chopped

2 carrots, chopped

4 thick slices of bacon, cut into thin strips

1 cup dry white wine

coarse sea salt and freshly ground black pepper

a roasting pan fitted with a rack

Serves 4

Rub the guinea fowl all over with 1 tablespoon of the olive oil and season well, inside and out. Put on a rack set in a roasting pan and cook in a preheated oven at 425°F until browned and the juices run clear when the thigh is pierced with a skewer, about 1 hour.

Meanwhile, put the lentils, thyme, and bay leaf in a saucepan and just cover with water. Bring to a boil, reduce the heat, cover with a lid, and simmer gently until tender, about 25 minutes. Drain and season with ½ teaspoon salt.

Heat the remaining 2 tablespoons oil in a skillet. Add the shallots and carrots and cook until just tender, 3–5 minutes. Add the bacon and cook, stirring, until well browned. Add the wine and cook over high heat until reduced by half. Add the lentils, discard the herbs, and set aside.

Remove the guinea fowl from the oven and let stand for 10 minutes. Carve into serving pieces and serve immediately, with the lentils.

Duck breasts are incredibly convenient—just a short time in the skillet and they can be served hot, as in this dish, or warm, as a salad served over baby spinach or watercress. This recipe goes well with sautéed or roasted potatoes and a red wine such as Madiran.

duck breasts with peppercorns
magret de canard aux deux poivres

2 duck breasts, about 1½ lb.

3 tablespoons Cognac

1 cup sour cream or crème fraîche

1 tablespoon coarsely ground black pepper

1 tablespoon green peppercorns in brine, drained

coarse sea salt

Serves 2

Trim the excess fat from around the duck breasts, then score the skin in a diamond pattern.

Heat a heavy skillet. When hot, add the duck skin side first and cook 7–8 minutes. Turn and cook the other side 4–5 minutes, depending on thickness. Remove from the pan, season with salt, and keep them warm.

Drain almost all the fat from the pan. Return to the heat and add the Cognac, scraping the bottom of the pan. Stir in the cream, black pepper, and green peppercorns. Warm through, but don't let the sauce boil.

Slice the duck diagonally lengthwise and put on plates. Pour the sauce over the top and serve immediately.

Rabbit and prunes don't really have a season, but this somehow seems autumnal, just the thing when the days are getting shorter and cooler, and it's nice to fill the house with appetizing aromas. A more apt name would be Drunken Rabbit, because there is so much wine, Cognac, and port. But prunes it is, and they do play a vital part, adding a pleasant sweetness to the rich, velvety sauce and salty bacon. Serve it with fresh pasta tossed in butter—tagliatelle is ideal. Chicken can be substituted for the rabbit, but don't cook it as long.

rabbit with prunes
lapin aux pruneaux

1 rabbit, cut into 7–8 pieces
2 tablespoons safflower oil
2 tablespoons unsalted butter
2 onions, halved and sliced
6 thick slices of bacon, cut into thin strips
about 1 cup all-purpose flour
½ cup port
2½ cups plump prunes, 12 oz.
1 tablespoon sour cream or crème fraîche
coarse sea salt and freshly ground black pepper

Marinade
1 onion, chopped
1 carrot, chopped
2 garlic cloves, crushed
2 sprigs of thyme
1 fresh bay leaf
1 bottle red wine, 750 ml
1 cup Cognac
a few peppercorns

Serves 4

One day before serving, mix all the marinade ingredients in a ceramic or glass bowl. Add the rabbit pieces, cover, and refrigerate overnight.

When ready to cook, remove the rabbit from the marinade, strain the liquid, and reserve. Discard all the vegetables but keep the thyme and bay leaf. Pat the rabbit pieces dry with paper towels.

Heat 1 tablespoon of the oil and 1 tablespoon of the butter in a casserole dish with a lid. Add the onions and bacon and cook over high heat until brown, 5 minutes. Pour off any excess fat, then remove the onions and bacon and set aside.

Put the flour on a plate and add the rabbit pieces, turning to coat lightly. Add the remaining oil and butter to the casserole and heat. When sizzling, put the rabbit pieces in the casserole and brown all over. Pour in the strained marinade liquid, bacon and onion mixture, and port. Add the reserved thyme and bay leaf and season with salt and pepper. Bring to a boil, skim off the foam, then lower the heat, cover, and simmer for 45 minutes. Taste for seasoning.

Remove the rabbit pieces to a plate, add the prunes, raise the heat, and cook until thickened, 10–15 minutes more. Stir in the sour cream, return the rabbit to the casserole, and cook just to warm through; do not boil. Serve immediately.

marinated pork roast
rôti de porc mariné

1 bottle dry white wine, 750 ml

2 cups white wine vinegar

1 large onion, sliced

2 carrots, sliced

1 fresh bay leaf

a sprig of thyme

1 celery stalk, with leaves

2 garlic cloves, sliced

1 teaspoon peppercorns

2 tablespoons coarse sea salt

2–3 fresh sage leaves

1 boneless pork loin roast, about 3 lb.

Serves 4–6

If you thought pork was bland, think again. It is actually a spectacular vehicle for all sorts of flavors, and responds remarkably well to marinating. The French have known this for years, because the idea for this recipe came from one of my favorite cookbooks, *La Cuisine de Mme Saint-Ange*, first published in 1927. Any cut of pork can be marinated, from a few hours to overnight, and the leftovers are as good, if not better, than the original. Serve with something creamy, like Cauliflower Gratin (page 109), or roasted vegetables.

Two days before serving, mix all the ingredients in a large ceramic or glass bowl. Cover and refrigerate for 2 days, turning the pork regularly.

When ready to cook, remove the pork from the marinade and put it in a roasting pan. Add the vegetables and flavorings from the marinade. Cook in a preheated oven at 400°F, basting occasionally with the marinade liquid, for 1½ hours. Serve immediately.

If it has apples and cream, then it must be from Normandy. The cider is a good clue as well, and it provides a luxuriously rich sauce for the long-simmered pork. Unlike recipes from more southerly realms, this is subtle and delicate, but no less powerful for its discretion. A good dish for all the family, as children (and adults) enjoy sweet things to accompany their meat. Serve with the cider used in cooking, or a red wine from the Loire.

pork in cider with potatoes and apples
porc au cidre aux deux pommes

2 tablespoons unsalted butter

2 onions, sliced

1 tablespoon safflower oil

1 fresh ham, about 3½ lb., fat trimmed

1½ quarts hard dry cider

2 sprigs of thyme

1¾ lb. medium new potatoes, peeled and halved lengthwise

½ cup heavy cream

coarse sea salt and freshly ground black pepper

Apples

5 tart baking apples, peeled, cored and sliced

4 tablespoons unsalted butter

Serves 4

Melt the butter in a large casserole dish with a lid. Add the onions and cook gently until softened but not browned, about 5 minutes. Remove the onions. Add the oil, raise the heat, add the fresh ham, and cook until browned all over. Remove and season well.

Add some of the cider, heat, and scrape the bottom of the pan. Return the meat, onions, remaining cider, and thyme. Season lightly with salt and pepper and bring to a boil. Boil for 1 minute, skim off any foam that rises to the surface, then lower the heat, cover, and cook in a preheated oven at 300°F for 4 hours. Turn the pork regularly, and taste and adjust the seasoning halfway through cooking.

One hour before the end of the cooking time, add the potatoes and continue cooking.

Remove from the oven, transfer the pork and potatoes to a plate, and cover with foil to keep it warm. Cook the sauce over high heat to reduce slightly, 10–15 minutes. Taste.

Meanwhile, to cook the apples, melt the butter in a large skillet, add the apples and cook over high heat until browned and tender, 5–10 minutes. Do not crowd the pan; use 2 pans if necessary.

To serve, slice the pork and arrange on plates with the potatoes and apples. Stir the cream into the sauce and serve immediately.

This is the sort of basic fare you'll find in cafés and bistros all over France. The mustardy-vinegary sauce is ideal with pork. Cornichons are the best part, so be sure to use the real thing. They must be small and, ideally, bottled in France. I've seen other tiny gherkins labeled as cornichons but, unless they come from France, they never taste as I expect. Serve with mashed potatoes.

pork chops with piquant sauce
côtes de porc charcutière

4 thick-cut pork chops

extra virgin olive oil

coarse sea salt and freshly ground black pepper

Mustard and vinegar sauce

¼ cup wine, dry white or red

1 cup fresh chicken stock, preferably organic

¼ cup tarragon or sherry vinegar

4 tablespoons unsalted butter

3 shallots, finely chopped

1 tablespoon all-purpose flour

2 teaspoons tomato paste

1 teaspoon coarse Dijon mustard

8 French cornichons, sliced into rounds

a sprig of tarragon, leaves stripped and chopped

a small handful of flat-leaf parsley, chopped

Serves 2–4

To make the sauce, put the wine and stock in a small saucepan. Bring to a boil for 1 minute, then stir in the vinegar. Set aside.

Melt the butter in another saucepan. Add the shallots and cook until soft, 3–5 minutes. Add the flour and cook, stirring for 1 minute. Add the warm stock mixture and tomato purée and mix well. Simmer gently for 15 minutes.

Meanwhile, to cook the pork chops, rub a ridged stovetop grill pan with the oil and heat on high. When hot, add the pork chops and cook for 4–5 minutes. Turn and cook the other side for 3–4 minutes. Remove from the heat and season on both sides with salt and pepper.

Stir the mustard, cornichons, tarragon, and parsley into the sauce and serve immediately, with the pork chops.

cassoulet

A classic from the southwest, adapted for those of us outside France. Do not let the long list put you off. This is actually quite easy: cook the beans, cook the meat stew, brown the duck and sausages, then put it all together. That's it. You do need good sausages, with as high a pork content as possible. Duck confit is sold canned in large supermarkets, or in good gourmet stores. You will also need several large pots, a large dish to cook it in, and very hungry friends.

Beans

1¾ lb. dried haricot beans

a thick slice of country ham

a piece of salt pork

1 carrot, chopped

1 fresh bay leaf

1 onion, studded with 2 cloves

4 whole garlic cloves

1 teaspoon salt

Meat

1 tablespoon extra virgin olive oil

1½ lb. spareribs

1½ lb. boneless lamb shoulder, cubed

1 onion, chopped

3 garlic cloves, crushed

2 cups canned chopped peeled tomatoes, 16 oz.

1 fresh bay leaf

2 quarts chicken stock, preferably organic

6 canned duck confit thigh pieces

10 Toulouse sausages or other pure pork sausages

bread crumbs

coarse sea salt and freshly ground black pepper

Serves 8

In the morning, one day before serving, put the beans in a bowl with plenty of cold water and let soak (they should soak for at least 6 hours, or start 2 days early and soak overnight).

Drain the beans. Put in a large saucepan with cold water to cover, bring to a boil, and simmer for 10 minutes. Drain. Return the beans to the pan and add the ham, pork, carrot, bay leaf, onion, and garlic. Cover with water by about 2 inches and bring to a boil. Lower the heat and simmer gently for 1 hour. Add the 1 teaspoon salt and continue cooking for 30 minutes more. Let cool, then refrigerate overnight; do not drain.

Meanwhile, to prepare the meat stew, heat the oil in a large skillet. Add the spareribs and lamb and sauté until brown. Add the onion and garlic and cook until just soft, about 3 minutes. Add the tomatoes, bay leaf, and stock. Season. Bring to a boil, skim off the foam, then lower the heat, cover, and simmer gently for 1½ hours. Add salt and pepper to taste. Let cool and refrigerate overnight.

The next day, about 3 hours before serving, discard the fat from the top of the stew. Remove the meat from the spareribs, return to the stew, and discard the bones. Bring the beans to room temperature (or warm slightly), drain and reserve the liquid. Season to taste.

Heat a large skillet, add the duck confit pieces, and sauté until browned. Remove, cut into 6–8 pieces and set aside. In the same pan, brown the sausages. Do not discard the cooking fat.

Now you are ready to assemble. Remove the pork rind and bacon from the beans and put in a large casserole dish. Top with one-third of the beans. Arrange the duck confit in the middle (so that you know where to find it when serving), and the sausages all around the edge. Spread the meat stew on top. Cover with the remaining beans. Spoon in some of the reserved bean liquid (you should just be able to see it), then sprinkle with a thin layer of bread crumbs. Pour in the duck and sausage fat. Cook in a preheated oven at 425°F for 30 minutes.

Reduce the heat to 375°F. Gently break up the crust on top, then spoon over some more bean liquid and sprinkle with more bread crumbs. Continue checking, about every 30 minutes or so, adding more liquid as necessary; be sure not to let the cassoulet dry out. When the crust is well browned and the cassoulet has cooked for 2 hours, remove from the oven.

Serve hot, with a portion of confit, the sausages, and plenty of beans for each guest.

Nothing says "bistro" better than this. The shallot butter is a fancy flourish; it is just as authentic to serve as is, with nothing more than Dijon mustard, for both the steak and the fries (but no ketchup, please!) The secret of cooking great fries is to use a good "floury" baking variety of potato and to cook them twice. They should be dry, rustling, crisp, and well seasoned.

steak and fries
steak frites

4 sirloin or rib eye steaks, about 10 oz. each, 1 inch thick

1 tablespoon safflower oil

coarse sea salt and freshly ground black pepper

Shallot butter

1 stick unsalted butter, softened

2 shallots, finely chopped

⅔ cup red wine

a large sprig of tarragon

several sprigs of flat-leaf parsley

1 teaspoon coarse sea salt

½ teaspoon coarsely ground black pepper

Fries

1 lb. potatoes, suitable for baking and frying

safflower oil, for frying

sea salt, to serve

a large saucepan with frying basket, or electric deep-fryer

Serves 4

To make the shallot butter, put about 2 tablespoons of the butter in a saucepan and melt over low heat. Add the shallots and cook until softened. Add the wine, bring to a boil, and cook until syrupy and the wine has almost completely evaporated. Set aside to cool.

Put the cooled shallots, remaining butter, tarragon, parsley, salt, and pepper in a small food processor and blend briefly. Transfer the mixture to a piece of parchment paper and shape into a log. Roll up and chill until firm.

To prepare the fries, peel the potatoes and cut into ¼-inch slices. Cut the slices into ¼-inch strips. Put into a bowl of ice water for at least 5 minutes. When ready to cook, drain and pat dry with paper towels.

Fill a large saucepan one-third full with the oil or, if using a deep-fryer, to the manufacturer's recommended level. Heat the oil to 375°F or until a cube of bread will brown in 30 seconds. Working in batches, put 2 large handfuls of potato strips into the frying basket, lower carefully into the oil, and fry for about 4 minutes. Remove and drain on paper towels. Repeat until all the strips have been cooked. Skim any debris off the top of the oil, reheat to the same temperature, then fry the strips for a second time until crisp and golden, about 2 minutes. Remove and drain on paper towels, then sprinkle with salt. Keep hot in the oven until ready to serve

To prepare the steaks, rub them on both sides with the oil. Heat a ridged stovetop grill pan. When hot, add the steaks and cook for 1½–2 minutes. Turn and cook the other side for 1–2 minutes. This will produce a rare steak. To produce a medium-rare steak, turn and cook again on both sides for 2–3 minutes more.

Remove from the pan and season both sides. Let stand for a few minutes. Serve with rounds of the butter and the fries.

The sailors who used to guide barges up and down the Rhône, from Arles to Lyon, were lucky men indeed. They invented this dish and, I assume, ate it often. If I were having my last supper, this would be it, with mashed potatoes, a green salad, and a good red Rhône wine.

braised steak with anchovies and capers
brouffade

4 thick rump steaks, about 10 oz. each

⅔ cup extra virgin olive oil

8 garlic cloves, crushed

a small handful of flat-leaf parsley, chopped

1 teaspoon coarsely ground black pepper

1 fresh bay leaf

a sprig of thyme

1 inner stalk of celery, with leaves

4 onions, halved and sliced

3 tablespoons capers, drained

12 cornichons, chopped

10 anchovies, finely chopped

1 tablespoon all-purpose flour

3 tablespoons red wine vinegar

Serves 4–6

One day before serving, mix the oil, garlic, parsley, pepper, bay leaf, thyme, and celery in a shallow dish. Add the steaks and turn to coat well with the mixture. Cover with plastic wrap and refrigerate overnight, turning at least twice.

Put the onions, capers, and cornichons in a bowl and toss well.

Put the anchovies and flour in a small bowl and blend well. Remove the meat from the marinade and stir in the anchovy mixture and vinegar.

Choose a lidded ovenproof casserole, deep and just wide enough to hold 2 steaks side-by-side. Put one-third of the onion mixture in the casserole and put 2 steaks on top. Spoon in half of the marinade, spreading it over the meat. Top with half the remaining onions, then the remaining steaks. Spoon over the rest of the marinade and top with the rest of the onions.

Pour in about 1 cup water. Cut a piece of parchment paper to about the diameter of the casserole and put this on top of the onions to help seal in all the juices. Cover with the lid and cook in a preheated oven at 300°F for 3 hours. Serve immediately.

This humble French culinary masterpiece rates high on the scale of life's little pleasures. It has no precise geographical origin—everyone makes it, and rightly so. The beef practically melts in your mouth and the broth is rich, sweet, and buttery from all the carrots. A prime candidate for potatoes, tagliatelle, or, even better, Macaroni Gratin (page 118). French Beans with Garlic (page 106) would also be delicious. Experiment with different cuts of beef— anything that will stand up to long, slow simmering.

braised beef brisket with carrots
boeuf aux carottes

2 tablespoons extra virgin olive oil

3 lb. brisket, rolled and tied by the butcher

3 lb. carrots

5 thick slices of bacon, cut into thin strips

1 onion, halved and sliced

2 garlic cloves, crushed

1 fresh bay leaf

a sprig of thyme

1 small leafy celery stalk

2 cups dry white wine

coarse sea salt and freshly ground black pepper

Serves 4–6

Heat 1 tablespoon of the oil in a large casserole dish. Add the meat and cook until browned on all sides. Transfer to a plate and sprinkle generously with salt.

Heat the remaining oil in the casserole, add the carrots and 1 teaspoon salt, and cook, stirring occasionally until brown, 3–5 minutes. Remove and set aside.

Put the bacon and onions in the casserole and cook over high heat until browned, 3–5 minutes. Pour off the excess fat.

Add the garlic, bay leaf, thyme, celery, beef, and carrots. Pour in the wine and add water almost to cover. Bring to a boil, skim, then cover with a lid and cook in a preheated oven at 300°F for 3 hours. Turn the meat over at least once during cooking.

Sprinkle with pepper and serve with your choice of accompaniments.

This classic dish is a reminder that true bistro food is not about expensive cuts, or elaborate sauces. In fact, the real recipe calls for leftover beef from a stew—home economy at its best. If you have any leftovers from the Braised Beef (page 83), then use them. It's also nice if you mix leftovers, like lamb and pork, with the beef. This summery dish is ideal for lunch or a light supper, served with a green salad and a light-medium red wine.

stuffed tomatoes
tomates farcies

2 tablespoons extra virgin olive oil

4 shallots, finely chopped

3 large garlic cloves, crushed

5 slices bacon, finely chopped

3 tablespoons dry white wine

12 large vine-ripened tomatoes (not beefsteak)

12 oz. ground beef

1 large egg

¼ cup bread crumbs

½ teaspoon herbes de provence

a handful of flat-leaf parsley, finely chopped

coarse sea salt and freshly ground black pepper

a baking dish, greased with 2 tablespoons olive oil

Serves 4–6

Heat the oil in a skillet. Add the shallots and garlic and cook until softened but not browned, 3–5 minutes. Stir in the bacon and sauté until just beginning to brown, about 3–5 minutes. Add the wine and cook until evaporated. Transfer to a bowl and let cool.

Slice off the tops of the tomatoes and set the tops aside. Carefully core and seed with a spoon. Pat the insides dry with paper towels and season with salt and pepper. Set aside.

Add the beef to the shallot mixture, then stir in the egg, bread crumbs, herbs, parsley, and 1 teaspoon salt. Cook a small piece of the stuffing mixture in a skillet, taste for seasoning, then add more salt if needed.

Fill the tomato shells with the beef mixture, mounding it at the top. Replace the tomato tops and arrange apart in the prepared baking dish. Cook in a preheated oven at 400°F until cooked through and browned, about 30 minutes.

Variations Another speciality from Provence, *les petits farcis* (little stuffed vegetables), can be made using the same stuffing to fill a variety of vegetables—zucchini, eggplant, and peppers are ideal, but you can also use artichokes and mushrooms. Provençal dishes often have a bread crumb topping, so add a handful of chopped fresh parsley, crushed garlic, and some grated Parmesan to fresh bread crumbs and sprinkle over the tops before baking.

Antoine-Augustin Parmentier introduced potatoes to the French public in the late 18th century, and this dish of ground beef nestled between two layers of creamy mashed potatoes is a tribute to him. Not as glamorous as a bridge over the Seine perhaps, but delicious nonetheless. The traditional recipe calls for leftover cooked beef, specifically stewed or boiled beef, so use that if you have some. The taste benefits from flavorful leftovers, but ground beef that has been well seasoned and cooked in a bit of wine comes a close second. Serve with a fruity red wine from the Loire.

beef and potato gratin
hachis parmentier

3 tablespoons unsalted butter or 2 tablespoons safflower oil

2 onions, chopped

2 garlic cloves

1½ lb. ground beef

3 slices bacon, finely chopped

½ cup dry white wine

a handful of flat-leaf parsley, chopped

a sprig of thyme, leaves stripped

2 tablespoons tomato paste

2 oz. freshly grated Gruyère cheese, about ¼ cup

coarse sea salt and freshly ground black pepper

Potato purée

4 lb. potatoes

1 fresh bay leaf

1 cup hot milk

1 stick unsalted butter, cut into pieces

sea salt

a baking dish, about 12 inches long, greased with butter

Serves 4–6

To prepare the purée, put the potatoes and bay leaf in a saucepan of cold water. Bring to a boil, add salt, and cook until tender. Drain.

Put the potatoes in a large bowl and mash coarsely with a wooden spoon. Using an electric mixer, gradually add the milk and butter, beating until the mixture is smooth. Add salt and beat well. If the potatoes are very dry, add more milk. Taste, then add more butter and/or salt as necessary and set aside.

Heat the butter in a skillet, add the onions, and cook over high heat until just brown, 3–5 minutes. Add the garlic, beef, and bacon and cook until almost completely browned. Add the wine and cook until almost evaporated. Stir in the parsley, thyme leaves, and tomato paste. Taste and adjust the seasoning with salt and pepper.

Spread half the potatoes in the prepared baking dish. Add the beef mixture and level with a spoon. Spread with the remaining potatoes. Sprinkle with the cheese and bake in a preheated oven at 400°F until golden, about 25–30 minutes.

Gasconnade refers to the anchovies and it is a traditional way of flavoring lamb in the southwest of France. The long, slow cooking in wine mellows the anchovies, making for an intensely rich sauce and very tender meat. Serve with fresh tagliatelle, potatoes, or flageolet beans.

leg of lamb
with anchovies
agneau à la gasconnade

1 leg of lamb, about 3 lb., trimmed

14 anchovies

2 tablespoons extra virgin olive oil

2 onions, chopped

2 carrots, chopped

3 garlic cloves, crushed

2 vine-ripened tomatoes, peeled, seeded, and chopped

1 bottle red wine, 750 ml

2 sprigs of thyme

1 fresh bay leaf

1 tablespoon tomato paste

coarse sea salt

Serves 4–6

Make slits all over the lamb and insert the anchovy fillets, as you do when studding with garlic.

Heat the oil in a lidded casserole dish just large enough to hold the lamb comfortably. Add the lamb and brown on all sides. Remove, season lightly, and set aside.

Put the onions and carrots in the casserole and cook over high heat until lightly browned, about 3–5 minutes. Add the garlic and tomatoes and cook for 1 minute. Add the wine, thyme, bay leaf, and tomato paste, bring to a boil for 1 minute, then add the lamb. Cover with the lid, transfer to a preheated oven at 350°F and cook for 1½ hours, turning every 20 minutes or so. Remove the thyme and bay and serve.

This reminds me of long Sunday family lunches, the ones that go on almost until dinner, the likes of which I'd never known before living in France. To recreate something similar, start with apéritifs and nibbles at midday, then serve this with boiled baby new potatoes and a bottle of St-Emilion. Follow with a green salad and a generous cheese platter. An apple tart (page 132) before coffee makes the perfect ending. A lovely way to herald in the spring.

spring lamb stew
with vegetables
navarin d'agneau

1 tablespoon safflower oil

1½ lb. boneless rib lamb chops, cubed

1 lb. boneless loin lamb chops, each one cut into several pieces

1 tablespoon all-purpose flour

2 vine-ripened tomatoes, peeled, seeded, and chopped

2 garlic cloves, crushed

2¾ cups fresh lamb or chicken stock, preferably organic

1 fresh bay leaf

a sprig of thyme

4 baby carrots, cut into 1-inch pieces

8 oz. baby leeks, cut into 2-inch lengths

8 oz. baby turnips

8 oz. sugar snap peas

a handful of flat-leaf parsley, chopped

coarse sea salt and freshly ground black pepper

Serves 4

Heat the oil in a large casserole dish, add the lamb, and brown on all sides, in batches if necessary. When all the lamb has been browned, return it all to the pan, lower the heat slightly, and stir in a pinch of salt and the flour. Cook, stirring to coat evenly, for 1 minute.

Add the tomatoes and garlic. Stir in the stock, bay leaf, and thyme. Bring to a boil and skim off any foam that rises to the surface. Reduce the heat, then cover and simmer gently for 40 minutes.

Add the carrots, leeks, and turnips and cook for 25 minutes more. Taste and adjust the seasoning with salt and pepper.

Add the peas and cook for 7 minutes. Sprinkle with the parsley and serve immediately.

vegetables

Poor old celery; it is more often an ingredient than the star of a dish. However, in this traditional Provençal recipe, it takes center stage. Beef is the ideal complement to the trinity of celery, tomatoes, and anchovies, so serve this with roast beef or grilled steaks.

braised celery
céleri braisé

2 whole bunches of celery

2 tablespoons extra virgin olive oil

2 thick slices of bacon, cut into thin strips

1 onion, halved, then quartered and sliced

1 carrot, halved lengthwise, then quartered and sliced

2 garlic cloves, sliced

1 cup canned chopped peeled tomatoes, 8 oz.

1 cup dry white wine

1 fresh bay leaf

8 canned anchovies, chopped

a handful of flat-leaf parsley, chopped

coarse sea salt and freshly ground pepper

Serves 4–6

Remove any tough outer stalks from the celery and trim the tips so they will just fit into a large sauté pan with a lid.

Bring a large saucepan of water to a boil. Add a pinch of salt, then the celery and simmer gently for 10 minutes to blanch. Remove, drain, and pat dry with paper towels.

Heat the oil in the sauté pan. Add the bacon, onion, and carrot and cook gently until lightly browned. Add the celery and a little salt and pepper and cook until just browned, then remove.

Add the garlic, cook for 1 minute, then add the tomatoes, wine, and bay leaf. Bring to a boil and cook for 1 minute. Add the celery, cover, and simmer gently for 30 minutes, turning the celery once during cooking.

Transfer the celery to a serving dish. Raise the heat and cook the sauce to reduce it slightly, about 10 minutes. Pour it over the celery, sprinkle with the anchovies and parsley, and serve.

Fresh peas with lettuce form a classic of French cuisine. Teamed with asparagus in a light buttery sauce, they're ideal for serving with roast poultry or grilled fish. Bacon makes a nice addition and you can also stir in ¼ cup finely chopped sautéed bacon, just before serving. If chervil is unavailable, use finely chopped flat-leaf parsley.

peas, asparagus, and baby lettuce

petits pois, asperges et laitues à la française

6 tablespoons unsalted butter

3–4 small shallots, sliced into rounds

2 romaine lettuce hearts, quartered

4 oz. asparagus tips, halved lengthwise

2 cups shelled fresh peas, 2 lb. in the pod

coarse sea salt

sprigs of chervil or chives snipped with kitchen shears, to serve

Serves 4

Melt half the butter in a saucepan with a lid. Add the shallots and lettuce and cook, covered, stirring often, until tender, 8–10 minutes.

Season with salt, add the remaining butter and asparagus and cook for 5 minutes.

Add the peas, cover, and cook for 3 more minutes. Taste for seasoning, sprinkle with the herbs, and serve.

Variation For a more substantial side dish, or even a light meal, add 10 oz. sliced baby carrots and a splash of water when cooking the lettuce. Before serving, gently stir in a bit more butter or 1 tablespoon crème fraîche and add 1 lb. boiled small new potatoes, sliced into wedges. Be sure to cook the potatoes in salted water or they will be bland.

Though pumpkin is not usually associated with French cooking, it is in fact a traditional ingredient. In the south of France, when it is in season, it often appears on menus as a gratin. The conventional recipe is simply a purée with béchamel and a topping of crisp, browned bread crumbs. This version has rice, which gives it a more interesting texture and makes it substantial enough to be a meal on its own, served with a green salad.

pumpkin and rice gratin
gratin de courge et de riz

3 lb. pumpkin

3 tablespoons extra virgin olive oil

½ cup long-grain rice

a sprig of thyme

3 tablespoons fresh bread crumbs

a small handful of flat-leaf parsley, finely chopped

3 tablespoons sour cream or crème fraîche

¾ cup finely grated Gruyère cheese, about 3 oz.

coarse sea salt and freshly ground black pepper

a large baking dish, greased with unsalted butter

Serves 6 as an entrée, 8 as a side dish

Peel and seed the pumpkin and cut into small cubes. Put in a large saucepan with 2 tablespoons of the oil, a pinch of salt, and 1 cup water. Cook over low heat, stirring often and adding more water as necessary, until soft, about 20–30 minutes.

Meanwhile, put the rice and the remaining 1 tablespoon oil in another saucepan and cook over medium heat, stirring to coat the grains. Add 1 cup water, a pinch of salt, and thyme and bring to a boil. Cover and simmer until almost tender, about 10 minutes, then drain and discard the thyme.

Mix the bread crumbs with the parsley and a pinch of salt.

Squash the cooked pumpkin into a coarse purée with a wooden spoon and stir in the rice and sour cream. Taste; the topping and cheese will add flavor, but the pumpkin should be seasoned with salt and pepper as well.

Spoon the pumpkin mixture into the prepared baking dish, spreading evenly. Sprinkle the cheese in a thin layer over the top, then follow with a layer of the bread crumbs. Bake in a preheated oven at 400°F until browned, about 20–30 minutes. Serve hot.

Cream and potatoes, mingling in the heat of the oven, are almost all you'll find in this well-loved dish. If it had cheese, it wouldn't be a true dauphinois. Serve on its own, with a mixed green salad, or as a partner for simple roast meat or poultry.

creamy potato gratin
gratin dauphinois

4¼ lb. boiling potatoes, cut in half if large

2 quarts whole milk

1 fresh bay leaf

2 tablespoons unsalted butter

2 cups whipping cream

a pinch of freshly grated nutmeg

coarse sea salt

a baking dish, 12 inches long

Serves 4–6

Put the potatoes in a large saucepan with the milk and bay leaf. Bring to a boil, then lower the heat, add a pinch of salt, and simmer gently until partially cooked, 5–10 minutes.

Drain the potatoes. When cool enough to handle (but still hot), slice into rounds about ⅛ inch thick.

Spread the butter in the the baking dish. Arrange half the potato slices in the dish and sprinkle with salt. Top with the remaining potato and more salt. Pour the cream over the top and sprinkle with grated nutmeg.

Bake in a preheated oven at 350°F until golden and the cream is almost absorbed, but not completely, about 45 minutes. Serve hot.

A meal in itself, this is very rich and filling, perfect after a day on the slopes. You might find this on menus in the Savoie region of France, though it is not, strictly speaking, a traditional recipe. It was "invented" in the 1980s by the local cheese committee to help sell more Reblochon cheese—and I'm sold!

potatoes baked with reblochon cheese
tartiflette

2¼ lb. boiling potatoes

I fresh bay leaf

4 tablespoons unsalted butter

2 onions, halved and sliced

5 thick slices bacon, thinly sliced

⅓ cup dry white wine

I Reblochon cheese, I lb.*

coarse sea salt and freshly ground black pepper

a baking dish, about 12 inches long, greased with butter

Serves 6

Put the potatoes in a large saucepan, then add the bay leaf and cold water to cover. Bring to a boil, add a handful of salt and cook until the potatoes are *al dente*, about 15 minutes. Drain. When cool enough to handle, peel and slice.

Melt half the butter in sauté pan, add the onions and bacon, and cook until just browned. Remove with a slotted spoon and reserve. Add the remaining butter and the potatoes and cook gently for 5 minutes. Stir carefully without breaking too many potato slices. Add the wine and bring to a boil for 1 minute. Season with salt and pepper.

Arrange the potatoes in the prepared baking dish. Scrub the rind of the cheese lightly with a vegetable brush, then cut into 8 wedges. Cut each piece in half through the middle, so each has skin on one side only. Arrange the cheese pieces on top of the potatoes, skin side up. Cover with foil and bake in a preheated oven at 425°F for about 15 minutes. Remove the foil and bake 15–20 minutes more, until browned. Serve hot.

*****Note** If Reblochon is unavailable, substitute any other French mountain cheese, such as Emmental, Cantal, or a Pyrénées. A firm goat cheese, such as Crottin de Chavignol, is also very nice. Alternatively, this recipe is a great way to clear out a cluttered cheese compartment, especially the post-dinner party syndrome of lovely but unfinished cheeses. Simply crumble or slice whatever you've got and put it on top of the potatoes before baking. It will no longer be tartiflette, but still very much in keeping with the bistro spirit of recycling leftovers.

Thyme is omnipresent in French cuisine. Here, it transforms what would otherwise be ordinary boiled carrots into something subtly sumptuous. The crème fraîche helps too. You can substitute steamed baby leeks for the carrots, but stir in a tablespoon or so of butter when adding the cream.

carrots with cream and herbs
carottes à la crème aux herbes

2 lb. baby carrots, trimmed, or medium carrots

3 tablespoons unsalted butter

a sprig of thyme

2 tablespoons sour cream or crème fraîche

several sprigs of chervil

a small bunch of chives

fine sea salt

Serves 4

If using larger carrots, cut them diagonally into 2-inch slices. Put in a large saucepan (the carrots should fit in almost a single layer for even cooking). Add the butter and set over low heat. Cook to melt and coat, about 3 minutes. Half fill the saucepan with water, then add a pinch of salt and the thyme. Cover and cook until the water is almost completely evaporated, 10–20 minutes.

Stir in the cream and add salt to taste. Using kitchen shears, snip the chervil and chives over the top, mix well, and serve.

Variation In spring, when turnips are sweet, they make a nice addition to this dish. Peel and quarter large turnips, or just peel baby ones—the main thing is to ensure that all the vegetable pieces (carrot and turnip) are about the same size so that they cook evenly. Halve the carrot quantity and complete with turnips, or double the recipe. Sprinkle with a large handful of just-cooked shelled peas before serving for extra crunch and pretty color.

French beans are the classic accompaniment for lamb, but they are equally nice with fish and chicken. You can also serve at room temperature, as part of a salad buffet. Instead of the cooked beans, try long, thin slices of steamed zucchini, sautéed with the garlic.

french beans with garlic
haricots verts à l'ail

1½ lb. small green beans, trimmed

2 tablespoons extra virgin olive oil

1 tablespoon unsalted butter

2 garlic cloves, crushed

a handful of flat-leaf parsley, chopped

1 teaspoon freshly squeezed lemon juice (optional)

coarse sea salt and freshly ground black pepper

Serves 4

Bring a large saucepan of water to a boil. Add the beans and cook for 3–4 minutes from the time the water returns to a boil. Drain and refresh under cold running water. Set aside.

Heat the oil and butter in a skillet. Add the garlic, beans, and salt and cook over high heat for 1 minute, stirring. Remove from the heat, then stir in the chopped parsley and lemon juice, if using. Sprinkle with pepper and serve.

Variation Flageolet beans are the other traditional partner for lamb. Generally, dried beans taste better if cooked from scratch, but this does require advance planning. Happily, I find that flageolets are the exception, especially if you can find imported French flageolets in jars, not cans. For mixed beans to serve with lamb (for four), halve the quantity of green beans and add a 14-oz. jar of drained beans to the cooked green beans when sautéing with the garlic. Instead of lemon juice, stir in 3–4 tablespoons crème fraîche or cream just before serving.

A regular accompaniment on the *plat du jour* circuit, this recipe goes especially well with pork. The secret of delicious cauliflower is to blanch it first; if you parboil it with a bay leaf, the unpleasant cabbage aroma disappears.

cauliflower gratin
gratin de chou-fleur

1 large cauliflower, separated into large florets

1 fresh bay leaf

2 cups heavy cream

1 large egg, beaten

2 teaspoons Dijon mustard

1½ cups finely grated Comté cheese, 6 oz.

coarse sea salt

a baking dish, about 10 inches diameter, greased with butter

Serves 4–6

Bring a large saucepan of water to a boil, add the bay leaf, salt generously, then add the cauliflower. Cook until still slightly firm, about 10 minutes. Drain and set aside.

Put the cream in a saucepan and bring to a boil. Boil for 10 minutes. Add a spoonful of hot milk to the beaten egg to warm it, then stir in the egg, mustard, and 1 teaspoon salt.

Divide the cauliflower into smaller florets, then stir into the cream sauce. Transfer to the prepared dish and sprinkle the cheese over the top in an even layer. Bake in a preheated oven at 400°F until golden, about 40–45 minutes. Serve hot.

Note Like Gruyère, Comté is a mountain cheese—from the Franche-Comté region to be precise—but the similarity stops there. Comté's distinct flavor comes from the milk used in the making, so the flavor varies with the seasons. A springtime diet of tender young shoots delivers milk that is very different from its winter counterpart, nourished mainly on hay. I've never met a Comté I didn't like, but it is darker in color and fruitier in summer, paler and more nutty in winter. Use Emmental or Cantal if it is unavailable, or see page 142 for French cheese websites.

Tian is the Provençal name for a square earthenware dish, but I use a nonstick roasting pan and the tian still tastes great. Ideally, it should be served tepid or at room temperature, as it would be for the sweltering heat of a Provençal summer. The tian will improve with age and can easily be made one day in advance.

eggplant, onion, and tomato tian

tian d'aubergine aux oignons et tomates

4 medium eggplant, sliced crosswise into 1-inch pieces

5 tablespoons fresh bread crumbs

½ teaspoon herbes de provence

about ½ cup extra virgin olive oil

2 large onions, sliced into thick rings

3 large vine-ripened tomatoes, sliced (not beefsteak)

¼ cup pitted black olives, sliced

coarse sea salt and freshly ground black pepper

Tomato sauce

1 tablespoon extra virgin olive oil

3 garlic cloves

3 lb. vine-ripened tomatoes, peeled, seeded, and chopped

a pinch of sugar

a small handful of basil, chopped

a small handful of flat-leaf parsley, chopped

coarse sea salt and freshly ground black pepper

nonstick roasting pan or earthenware dish

Serves 4–6

To make the tomato sauce, heat the oil in a saucepan, add the garlic, and cook until just soft, 1–2 minutes. Add the tomatoes, sugar, and salt to taste. Cover and simmer gently for 10 minutes. Stir in the basil and parsley and set aside.

Bring a large saucepan of water to a boil and add a pinch of salt. Add the eggplant slices and cook until just blanched and tender, 3–5 minutes. Drain well.

Put the bread crumbs, herbs, and a pinch of salt in a bowl, stir well, and set aside.

Pour 3–4 tablespoons of the oil in the baking dish, arrange the eggplant rounds on top, and pour over some of the remaining oil. Top with the onion rings and sprinkle with salt and pepper. Dot the sauce on top, spreading as evenly as possible. Arrange the tomato slices on top, sprinkle with the bread crumbs, followed by the olives. Bake in a preheated oven at 400°F until well browned, about 45 minutes. Serve hot or warm.

I first learned to make ratatouille from a friend's mother in her kitchen in Aix-en-Provence. Her method involves adding each vegetable separately, in the order which best suits their cooking requirements. It does make a difference because I've rarely tasted a ratatouille as good. It is also important to season each vegetable "layer" individually. Finally, I prefer my ratatouille vegetables to be distinct from each another, so cut the pieces medium-large, about 1½ inches thick. Serve with crusty bread.

ratatouille

2 lb. eggplant, cut into pieces

extra virgin olive oil (see method)

2 medium onions, coarsely chopped

2 red bell peppers, halved, seeded, and cut into pieces

2 yellow bell peppers, halved, seeded, and cut into pieces

1 green bell pepper, halved, seeded, and cut into pieces

6 smallish zucchini, about 1½ lb., halved lengthwise and sliced

4 garlic cloves, crushed

6 medium vine-ripened tomatoes, halved, seeded, and chopped

a small bunch of basil, coarsely chopped

coarse sea salt

To serve

a few basil leaves, finely sliced

1 garlic clove, crushed

Serves 4–6

Put the eggplant pieces in a microwave-proof bowl with 3 tablespoons water and microwave on HIGH for 6 minutes. Drain and set aside.

Heat 3 tablespoons of the oil in a deep sauté pan with a lid. Add the onions and cook until soft, 3–5 minutes. Salt lightly.

Add all the peppers and cook for 5–8 minutes more, stirring often. Turn up the heat to keep the sizzling sound going, but take care not to let it burn. Salt lightly.

Add 1 more tablespoon of the oil and the zucchini. Mix well and cook for about 5 minutes more, stirring occasionally. Salt lightly.

Add 2 more tablespoons of the oil and the drained eggplant. Cook, stirring often, for 5 minutes more. Salt lightly.

Add the garlic and cook for 1 minute. Add 1 more tablespoon of the oil if necessary, and the tomatoes and basil and stir well. Salt lightly. Cook for 5 minutes, then cover, lower the heat, and simmer gently for 30 minutes, checking occasionally.

Remove from the heat. This is best served at room temperature, but it still tastes nice hot. The longer you let it stand, the richer it tastes. Stir in more basil and garlic just before serving.

There are several regional variations on this recipe and it was difficult to choose which one to include. *Chou rouge à la flammande* has apples, *à la limousine* has chestnuts. This has it all, with some Alsatian Riesling and bacon as well—serve it with grilled sausages, pork chops, or roasts, and the same wine as used in the cooking. It is also fantastic with Christmas goose.

braised red cabbage
with chestnuts and apples
chou rouge aux marrons et aux pommes

I red cabbage

3 tablespoons unsalted butter

I onion, halved and thinly sliced

5 thick slices bacon, cut into thin slices

3 baking apples, peeled, cored, and chopped

7 oz. vacuum-packed whole peeled chestnuts

2 teaspoons coarse sea salt

I cup dry white wine, preferably Riesling

I tablespoon sugar

Serves 4–6

Cut the cabbage in quarters, then core and slice thinly.

Melt 2 tablespoons of the butter in a sauté pan. Add the onion and bacon and cook until soft, about 3 minutes.

Add the remaining butter, the cabbage, apples, and chestnuts and stir well. Season with salt, then add the wine, sugar, and I cup water.

Bring to a boil for I minute, then cover and simmer gently until the cabbage is tender, about 45 minutes.

Years ago, my husband and I went on a wine-buying mission with some friends in the Jura region of France. We stopped for lunch at a small hotel, but it was very late in the day, so we had to take what we were given. The offering was roast pork, served with a glorious mixture of vegetables, all thinly sliced and baked in a fabulous savory custard. Back home, I tried a similar dish using just spinach, because that's what was on hand, and it proved a great success.

spinach flan
flan d'épinards

I lb. fresh spinach

3–5 tablespoons extra virgin olive oil

¼ cup sour cream or crème fraîche

2 large eggs

I teaspoon coarse sea salt

a pinch of freshly grated nutmeg

I tablespoon unsalted butter

a baking dish, 12 inches long

Serves 4

Wash the spinach, then spin-dry in a salad spinner. Working in batches, heat I tablespoon of the oil in a nonstick skillet and add a mound of spinach. Cook the spinach over high heat, stirring until all the leaves have just wilted. Transfer to a plastic colander and let drain. Continue cooking until all the spinach has been wilted.

Chop the spinach coarsely. Put the sour cream, eggs, salt, and nutmeg in a bowl and beat well. Stir in the spinach.

Spread the butter in the bottom of a baking dish. Transfer the spinach mixture to the dish and bake in a preheated oven at 350°F until just set, 25–30 minutes. Serve hot.

This bistro classic is a much more sophisticated version of macaroni and cheese. It is ideal for serving with beef stews, as the gratin is even better when mixed with broth.

macaroni gratin
gratin de macaroni

10 oz. thin macaroni

2 cups milk

3 tablespoons sour cream or crème fraîche

4 tablespoons unsalted butter

¼ cups all-purpose flour

coarse sea salt and freshly ground black pepper

1⅔ cups finely grated Beaufort cheese, 7 oz.*

a baking dish, 12 inches long, greased with butter

Serves 6

Cook the macaroni in plenty of boiling, well-salted water according to the instructions on the package. Drain, rinse well, and return to the empty saucepan.

Heat the milk in a saucepan and stir in the sour cream. Melt the butter in a second saucepan over medium-high heat. Stir in the flour and cook, stirring constantly for 3 minutes. Pour in the milk mixture and stir constantly until the mixture thickens. Season with salt and pepper.

Stir the milk mixture into the macaroni and taste, adding salt and pepper if necessary. Transfer to the baking dish and sprinkle with the cheese. Cook under a preheated broiler until bubbling and browned, 10–15 minutes. Serve hot.

*Note Beaufort is an alpine cheese, similar to Gruyère, but with a slightly sweeter, more pronounced nutty flavor. It is becoming more widely available outside France, but if you cannot find it, Emmental, Cantal, or any firm, Cheddar-like cheese will do. The taste will be entirely different, of course.

sweet things

As soon as it's strawberry season, you'll find this on menus all over France, though Plougastel in Brittany claims to be home to the best of the French strawberry crop. Wherever they come from, lemon juice is key, enhancing the flavor of the fruit as well as adding tartness to show off the sugar. Be sure to taste before adding all the lemon juice; the amount can vary depending on the quality of the strawberries. This is as much blueprint as recipe so, once you've made it the traditional way, try it other ways. Use orange or lime juice instead of lemon and sprinkle with a small handful of chopped fresh mint leaves, for example. You can also serve it with slices of poundcake or rolled into crêpes, and pass the whipped cream or vanilla ice cream.

sugared strawberries
fraises au sucre

2 pints strawberries, at room temperature

freshly squeezed juice of 1 lemon

3–5 tablespoons sugar

crème fraîche or whipped cream, to serve

Serves 4–6

Trim the strawberries and put in a pretty bowl. Add the lemon juice and 3 tablespoons of the sugar. Mix gently but thoroughly and let stand about 15 minutes. Taste, and add more sugar if necessary.

This dish improves with standing, but don't leave it too long. If you make it just before you're ready to begin your meal, it will be ready in time for dessert.

If using crème fraîche, sweeten it with a spoonful of sugar.

Variation Peach or nectarine slices can be substituted for the strawberries, if you like to stick to single fruit, or use a mixture of soft fruit including red currants, blueberries, raspberries, and blackberries.

These are neither too sweet, nor too heavy; the perfect ending to a substantial bistro-style meal. Preparation is simple, but there are a few tricks to facilitate unmolding. First, don't use molds that are too deep (and don't overfill them). Then, let the custards stand in the bain-marie for a good 15 minutes before removing them to cool completely. According to a reliable old French cookbook of mine, this allows the custard to settle and solidify, making it easier to turn out. Just before serving, run a knife around the inside edge, hold an upturned plate over the top and flip over to release the custard.

caramel custard
crème renversée au caramel

3 cups whole milk

1 vanilla bean, split lengthwise with a small sharp knife

¾ cup plus 2 tablespoons sugar

5 large eggs

a pinch of salt

8 ramekins, 3 inches diameter

a roasting pan to hold the ramekins

Serves 8

Put the milk, vanilla bean, and its seeds in a saucepan and bring to a boil over medium heat. Immediately remove from the heat, cover, and let stand while you make the caramel.

To make the caramel, put ½ cup of the sugar and ¼ cup water in a small heavy saucepan, preferably with a pouring lip. Heat until the sugar turns a deep caramel color. Remove from the heat. When it stops sizzling, pour carefully into the ramekins. Take care not to let the caramel come into contact with your skin; it is very hot. Set the ramekins in a roasting pan and add boiling water to come halfway up the sides—this is called a bain-marie. Set aside.

Add the remaining 6 tablespoons sugar and the salt to the saucepan of warm milk and stir until dissolved. Remove the vanilla bean.

Crack the eggs into another bowl and whisk until smooth. Pour the warm milk into the eggs and stir well. Ladle into the ramekins.

Carefully transfer the bain-marie with the ramekins into a preheated oven at 350°F and bake until the custard is set and a knife inserted into the middle comes out clean, about 20–25 minutes. Serve at room temperature either in the ramekins or inverted onto plates so the caramel forms a pool of sweet sauce.

This is very easy to make and ideal for entertaining, since it should be made one day in advance. It is also deceptively rich, thanks to the egg yolks, which could also be reduced in quantity or omitted altogether. It is important to use good-quality chocolate, but anything over 70 percent cocoa solids will be too much. In traditional bistros, chocolate mousse is often served in a single, large bowl and passed around the table for diners to help themselves, so if you're expecting a crowd, double the recipe and do the same.

chocolate mousse
mousse au chocolat

7 oz. bittersweet chocolate, broken into pieces

2 tablespoons unsalted butter, cut into small pieces

1 vanilla bean, split lengthwise with a small sharp knife

3 large eggs, separated

a pinch of salt

2 tablespoons sugar

whipped cream, to serve (optional)

Serves 4

Put the chocolate in a glass bowl and melt in the microwave on HIGH for 40 seconds. Remove, stir, and repeat until almost completely melted. Remove, then stir in the butter. Using the tip of a small knife, scrape the small black seeds from the vanilla bean into the chocolate. Add the egg yolks, stir, and set aside.

Using an electric mixer, beat the egg whites and salt until foaming. Continue beating and add the sugar. Beat on high until glossy and firm.

Carefully fold the whites into the chocolate with a rubber spatula until no more white specks can be seen.

Transfer the mousse to serving dishes and refrigerate for at least 6 hours, but overnight is best. Serve with whipped cream.

This is a very simple, classic recipe and there are hundreds of versions. Some cook on top of the stove, some call for long-grain rice, some add eggs or egg yolks, and some add flavorings such as orange peel or cinnamon. One thing that is fairly consistent among French recipes is the double rice-cooking method and the reason is that blanching the rice first removes much of the starch. The result is light and delicate, not blobby and glutinous like some puddings I've tasted. The list of things to serve with it is fairly unlimited. Cooked and puréed apples or apricots, red fruit coulis, chocolate sauce, and custard sauce are traditional, but the American in me likes cranberry sauce. Of course, the pudding is also very nice just as it is.

rice pudding
riz au lait

½ cup risotto rice, such as arborio

2 cups whole milk, boiled

⅓ cup sugar

1 vanilla bean, split lengthwise with a small sharp knife

1 tablespoon unsalted butter

a pinch of salt

Serves 4

Put the rice in a saucepan with a lid and add cold water to cover. Slowly bring to a boil over medium heat, then boil for 5 minutes. Drain the rice and rinse under cold water. Set aside to drain well.

Meanwhile, put the milk in an ovenproof saucepan with a lid and bring to a boil. Add the sugar and vanilla bean. Remove from the heat, cover, and let stand for 15 minutes. Using the tip of the knife, scrape out the vanilla seeds and stir them through the milk.

Add the rice to the milk, then add the butter and salt. Bring slowly to a boil. Cover and transfer to a preheated oven at 350°F. Do not stir. Cook until the rice is tender and the liquid is almost completely absorbed but not dry, about 25–35 minutes. Serve warm.

In early summer, many bistro menus feature clafoutis, a custard-like batter baked with whole cherries and a speciality of the Limousin region. It is one of the finest French desserts, and a cinch to make. The only drawback is that the cherry season is a short one, and it is a shame to limit clafoutis making to just one part of the year. Plums, pears, and apples work well as substitutes, but rhubarb is fantastic. Almost better than the original, I think.

rhubarb clafoutis
clafoutis à la rhubarbe

1 lb. fresh rhubarb, cut into thick slices

¾ cup whole milk

¾ cup heavy cream

3 large eggs

¾ cup sugar

¼ teaspoon ground cinnamon

a pinch of salt

1 vanilla bean, split lengthwise with a small sharp knife

⅓ cup all-purpose flour

a large baking dish, about 12 inches diameter, greased with butter and sprinkled with sugar

Serves 6

Bring a saucepan of water to a boil, add the rhubarb, and cook for 2 minutes, just to blanch. Drain and set aside.

Put the milk, cream, eggs, sugar, cinnamon, and salt in a bowl and mix well. Using the tip of a knife, scrape the vanilla seeds into the mixture. Add the flour and beat well.

Arrange the rhubarb pieces in the prepared dish. Pour the batter over the top and bake in a preheated oven at 400°F until puffed and golden, about 40–45 minutes.

Golden Delicious is the apple of preference for most French dishes. It's not an especially interesting eating variety, but it's perfect for baking and cooking. It holds its shape well and is not too tart. The vanilla-scented purée is an extra, but well worth the indulgence.

simple apple tart
tarte aux pommes

1½ cups all-purpose flour, plus extra for rolling

1 tablespoon sugar

7 tablespoons cold unsalted butter, cut into pieces

a pinch of salt

Apple purée

3 Golden Delicious apples, peeled and chopped

1 vanilla bean, split lengthwise with a small sharp knife

2 tablespoons sugar

1 tablespoon unsalted butter

Apple topping

3 Golden Delicious apples, peeled and sliced

1 tablespoon unsalted butter, melted

1 tablespoon sugar

parchment paper and beans or baking weights

a tart pan with removable base, 11 inches diameter, greased and floured

Serves 6

To make the dough, put the flour, sugar, butter, and salt in a food processor and, using the pulse button, process until the butter is broken down (5–10 pulses). Add 3 tablespoons cold water and pulse just until the dough forms coarse crumbs; add 1 more tablespoon if necessary, but do not do more than 10 pulses.

Transfer the dough to a sheet of parchment paper, form into a ball, and flatten to a disk. Wrap in the parchment and refrigerate for 30–60 minutes.

Roll out the dough on a floured work surface to a disk slightly larger than the tart pan. Carefully transfer the dough to the pan, patching any holes as you go and pressing gently into the sides. To trim the edges, roll a rolling pin over the top, using the edge of the pan as a cutting surface, and let the excess fall away. Tidy up the edges and refrigerate until firm, about 30–60 minutes.

Prick the dough all over and line with the parchment paper and fill with beans or baking weights. Bake in a preheated oven at 400°F for 15 minutes, then remove the paper and weights and bake until just golden, about 10–15 minutes more. Let the tart crust cool slightly before filling.

To make the apple purée, put the chopped apples, vanilla bean, sugar, and butter in a saucepan, add ¼ cup water, and cook gently, stirring often until soft, adding more water if necessary, about 10–15 minutes. Use the tip of a small knife to scrape the seeds out of the vanilla bean into the purée, then discard the pod. Transfer the mixture to a food processor, blender, or food mill and purée. Alternatively, use a potato masher.

Spread the purée evenly in the tart shell. Arrange the apple slices in a circle around the edge; they should be slightly overlapping but not completely squashed together. Repeat for an inner circle, trimming the slices slightly so they fit, and going in the opposite direction from the outer circle. Brush with the melted butter and sprinkle with the sugar. Bake in a preheated oven at 400°F until just browned and tender, about 25–35 minutes. Serve warm or at room temperature.

This is elegant, both in appearance and flavor. It is ideal for entertaining since the tart crust and almond cream can be made a few hours in advance. To make it even more special, serve with crème fraîche sweetened with some sugar, or good-quality vanilla ice cream.

pear and almond tart
tarte aux poires frangipane

1½ cups all-purpose flour, plus extra for rolling

2 teaspoons sugar

7 tablespoons cold unsalted butter, cut into pieces

a pinch of salt

3–4 ripe pears*

Almond cream

7 tablespoons unsalted butter

½ cup sugar

2 large eggs

½ cup ground almonds, or slivered almonds ground to a powder

2 tablespoons all-purpose flour

parchment paper and beans or baking weights

a tart pan with removable base, 11 inches diameter, greased and floured

Serves 6

*If only unripe pears are available, poach them for 5 minutes in a saucepan of water with the freshly squeezed juice of ½ lemon.

To make the dough, put the flour, sugar, butter, and salt in a food processor and, using the pulse button, process until the butter is broken down (about 5–10 pulses). Add 3 tablespoons cold water and pulse until the dough forms coarse crumbs; add 1 more tablespoon if necessary, but do not do more than 10 pulses.

Transfer the dough to a sheet of parchment paper, form into a ball, and flatten to a disk. Wrap in paper and let stand for 30–60 minutes.

Roll out the dough on a floured work surface to a disk slightly larger than the tart pan. Carefully transfer the dough to the pan, patching any holes as you go and pressing gently into the sides. To trim the edges, roll a rolling pin over the top, using the edge of the pan as a cutting surface, and let the excess fall away. Tidy up the edges and refrigerate until firm, about 30–60 minutes.

Prick the dough all over, line with the parchment paper, and fill with beans or baking weights. Bake on a low shelf in a preheated oven at 400°F for 15 minutes, then remove the paper and weights and bake until just golden, about 10–15 minutes more. Let the tart crust cool slightly before filling. Lower the oven temperature to 375°F.

Meanwhile, to make the almond cream, put the butter and sugar in a bowl and beat with an electric mixer until fluffy and lemon-colored. Beat in the eggs, one at a time. Using a spatula, fold in the almonds and flour until well mixed. Spread the almond cream evenly in the tart crust.

Peel and slice the pears, into 8 or 12 slices, depending on the size of the pears. Arrange the pear slices on top of the almond cream.

Bake until puffed and golden, about 20–25 minutes. Serve warm.

When my son was little, we spent two weeks every September in a small village near Bandol, on the Mediterranean. The Sunday morning market was fantastic, but my favorite stall was held by a local farm woman, who sold fresh eggs, tree-ripened fruit, herbs and jars of the most delicious homemade jams I've ever tasted. The best was peach and red currant, a match made in heaven, so I've adapted a classic apple tart recipe in her honor. If you can't find red currants, use fresh blueberries instead.

peach and red currant tart
tarte aux pêches et aux groseilles

1½ cups all-purpose flour, plus extra for rolling

2 teaspoons sugar

7 tablespoons cold unsalted butter, cut into pieces

a pinch of salt

3–4 tablespoons cold water

Peach and red currant filling

3 large eggs

3 tablespoons sour cream or crème fraîche

¼ cup sugar

3 large ripe peaches, thinly sliced

4–5 stems of red currants, about 2 oz.

a tart pan with removable base, 11 inches diameter, greased and floured

parchment paper and baking beans or weights

Serves 12

To make the dough, put the flour, sugar, butter, and salt in a food processor and, using the pulse button, process until the butter is broken down (about 5–10 pulses). Add 3 tablespoons of the cold water and pulse just until the dough forms coarse crumbs; add 1 more tablespoon if necessary, but don't do more than 10 pulses.

Transfer the dough to a sheet of parchment paper, form into a ball, and flatten to a disk. Wrap in the paper and let stand for 30–60 minutes.

Roll out the dough on a floured work surface to a disk slightly larger than the tart pan. Carefully transfer the dough to the prepared pan, patching any holes as you go, and pressing gently into the sides. To trim the edges, roll a rolling pin over the top, using the edge of the pan as a cutting surface, and let the excess fall away. Tidy up the edges and refrigerate until firm, 30–60 minutes.

Preheat the oven to 400°F. Prick the dough all over, line with parchment paper, and fill with baking beans or weights. Bake for 15 minutes, then remove the parchment paper and weights, and bake until just golden, 10–15 minutes more. Let the tart crust cool slightly before filling. Leave the oven on.

To make the filling, put the eggs, sour cream or crème fraîche, and sugar in a bowl and beat well. Arrange the peach slices in 2 circles inside the cooled tart crust. The inner circle should go in the opposite direction from the outer circle. Pour in the egg mixture and sprinkle the red currants on top.

Bake until puffed and just beginning to brown, 25–30 minutes. Serve warm or at room temperature.

Any bistro worthy of the name will have a chocolate cake on its menu. This one is special because of the hazelnuts— a grown-up version of Nutella.

chocolate-hazelnut cake
gâteau au chocolat et aux noisettes

⅔ cup shelled hazelnuts, 3 oz.

5 oz. bittersweet chocolate, broken into pieces

5 tablespoons unsalted butter

⅔ cup sugar

4 large eggs, separated

¾ cup all-purpose flour

a pinch of salt

¼ cup sour cream or crème fraîche

whipped cream or crème fraîche, sweetened, to serve

To decorate

2 oz. semisweet chocolate, in once piece

1 tablespoon confectioners' sugar

1 tablespoon cocoa powder

a cake pan, 10 inches diameter, greased

Serves 8

Put all but 2 tablespoons of the hazelnuts in a small food processor and grind to a powder. Set aside.

Put the chocolate and butter in a glass bowl and microwave on HIGH for about 1½ minutes until almost completely melted. Stir, then let stand until fully melted.

Reserve 1 tablespoon of sugar and put the remainder in a large bowl. Add the egg yolks, then beat until fluffy and lemon-colored. Stir in the chocolate mixture, flour, salt, ground hazelnuts, and sour cream. The mixture will be slightly stiff.

Put the egg whites in another clean, grease-free bowl and beat with an electric hand mixer until frothy. Add the reserved 1 tablespoon sugar and beat on high until they hold stiff peaks. Using a rubber spatula, fold one-third of the egg whites into the chocolate mixture. Add the remaining whites, folding just until there are no more specks of white.

Transfer to the prepared cake pan and bake in a preheated oven at 350°F until a knife inserted in the middle comes out clean, 20–30 minutes. Let cool slightly, then invert onto a wire rack to cool.

To decorate, toast the remaining hazelnuts in a dry skillet, then crush lightly. Microwave the chocolate on HIGH for 30 seconds, then shave off curls with a vegetable peeler. Set aside. Put the confectioners' sugar and cocoa in a strainer and hold it over the cake. Tap the edge of the strainer to release the mixture, moving around the cake to coat. A very light dusting is sufficient. Sprinkle the chocolate and toasted hazelnuts in the center. Serve at room temperature, with lots of sweetened whipped cream or crème fraîche. The cake will keep well for several days in an airtight container.

Strictly speaking, this is more home cooking than bistro, but the line is a fine one and this recipe is too good not to include. The ½-cup yogurt pot is the measure, so it doesn't really matter what flavor—you use, but plain yogurt is my preference. If you don't fancy orange, try other flavorings: cinnamon, honey, vanilla, chocolate, fruit pieces … This is great to make, and eat, with children.

yogurt cake
gâteau au yaourt

½ cup plain set yogurt
1 cup sugar
1½ cups flour
2 large eggs
1 tablespoon safflower oil
1 teaspoon baking soda
a pinch of salt
freshly squeezed juice of 1 orange
1 tablespoon confectioners' sugar, to decorate

a deep cake pan, 9 inches diameter, greased

Serves 8

Empty the yogurt into a large bowl and wipe out the pot so when you measure the other ingredients, they won't stick. Otherwise, just use regular measuring cups. Add the sugar, flour, eggs, oil, baking soda, salt and half the orange juice. Stir well.

Pour into the prepared cake pan and bake in a preheated oven at 350°F until a knife inserted in the middle comes out clean, about 15–20 minutes. Remove from the oven and pierce a few holes in the top with a fork. Pour over the remaining orange juice. Let cool slightly, then turn out onto a wire rack to cool.

To decorate, put the confectioners' sugar in a strainer and hold it over the cake. Tap the edge of the strainer to release the sugar, moving around the cake to coat. A very light dusting is sufficient. Serve at room temperature.

mail order and websites

INTERNATIONAL INGREDIENTS

www.cheese.com
Index of 652 cheeses, classified by name, country, texture, and milk

www.france-gourmet.com
Very good selection of French cheeses.

www.frenchfeast.com
Good selection of gourmet French items including confit, beans for cassoulet, cornichons, lovely vinegars, goose fat, nut oils, harissa.

www.idealcheese.com
Crème fraîche imported from France, plus limited selection of French cheeses.

www.ilovecheese.com
User-friendly website of the American Dairy Association: recipes from leading US chefs, food and wine pairing suggestions, and home tasting "kits."

Penzeys Spices
P.O. Box 933
Muskego, WI 53150
800-741-7787
www.penzeys.com
All baking spices and extracts.

Sopexa: Food & Wines From France
www.frenchwinesfood.com
Providing useful links to many French food and wine sites.

Zingerman's Mail Order
620 Phoenix Drive
Ann Arbor, MI 48108
888-636-8162
www.zingermans.com
Gourmet store: mail order service.

WINE

Kermit Lynch Wine Merchant
1605 San Pablo Ave.
Berkeley, CA 94702
Tel: (510) 524-1524
Fax: (510) 528-7026
Email: klwm@earthlink.net
Importers of fine French country wines. Distributors nationwide.

ORGANIC MEATS, POULTRY, FISH, AND VEGETABLES

Browne Trading Company
Merrill's Wharf, 260 Commercial Street
Portland, Maine 04101
Tel: 207-766-2403
Fax: 207-766-2404
Mail order: 800-944-7848
www.browne-trading.com
Superb fresh fish and shellfish, caviar, and smoked salmon by mail order.

D'Artagnan
280 Wilson Avenue
Newark N.J. 07105
Tel: (800) 327-8246
Fax: (973) 465-1870
www.dartagnan.com
Suppliers of organic duck, guinea hen and rabbit and other quality meats. Also have confit and cornichons.

Eberly Poultry
1095 Mt Airy Road
Stevens, PA 17578
Tel: 717-336-6440
Fax: 717-336-6905
www.eberlypoultry.com
Top-quality organic chicken, duck, geese, gamebirds, and rabbits.

Le Gourmet Lorrain Inc.
(301) 772-3366
Suppliers of Chef Alain products, notably Toulouse sausages for cassoulet. Telephone orders only.

Niman Ranch
Marin County, California
Tel: 510-808-0340
www.nimanranch.com
Top-quality beef, pork, and lamb. Shipped fresh, never frozen. Available online and at gourmet food stores country-wide. Check website for distributors.

Pipestone Family Farms
Pipestone, Minnesota
Tel: 866-767-8875
www.pipestonefamilyfarms.com
Cooperative venture of over 250 hog farmers offering quality pork products.

Prather Ranch
Macdoel, California
Tel: 877-570-2333
www.pratherranch.com
Certified organic beef available online and at farmers' markets in the Northern California and Southern Oregon areas. Call for a schedule.

Urban Organic
Tel: 888-428-8680
www.urbanorganic.net
The largest organic produce home delivery service in America.

Wild Edibles
89 East 42nd Street
(inside Grand Central Station)
New York, NY 10017-5503
Tel: 212-687-4255
Retail store with fresh fish and shellfish.

SALAD PLANTS AND SEEDS

The Cook's Garden
Tel: 800-457-9703
www.cooksgarden.com
Organic seeds, plants, and supplies for culinary herbs and vegetables.

The Natural Gardening Company
P.O. Box 750776
Petaluma, CA 94975-0776
Tel: 707-766-9303
Fax: 707-766-9747
www.naturalgardening.com
The oldest certified organic nursery in the US. A source for plants and seeds.

Penn Herb Co., Ltd
603 North 2nd Street
Philadelphia, PA 19123
Tel: 800-523-9971
Fax: 215-632-7945
www.pennherb.com

Richters
357 Highway 47
Goodwood, Ontario,
Canada L0C 1A0
Tel: 905-640-6677
Fax: 905-640-6641
www.richters.com
Herb specialists.

Seeds of Changes
Tel: 888-762-7333
www.seedsofchange.com
Organic garden seeds and plants.

Shepherd's Garden Seeds
Tel: 800-503-9626
www.whiteflowerfarm.com
Seed division of perennial nursery with good selection of heirloom tomatoes.

BAKEWARE AND UTENSILS

The Baker's Catalogue
King Arthur Flour Company
PO Box 876,
Norwich, VT 05055-0876.
Tel 1-800-827-6836.
www.kingarthurflour.com
Bakeware and utensils, baker's equipment, and ingredients. Available mail order, on-line, or from their store.

Dean & Deluca
560 Broadway
New York, NY 10012
and other locations nationwide
Tel 800-221-7714
www.deanandeluca.com
Speciality bakeware and equipment plus ingredients. Mail order available.

Professional Cutlery Direct
Tel 1-800-859-6994
www.cutlery.com

Sur la Table
2 dozen stores nationwide
Tel 1-800 243 0852
www.surlatable.com

Williams-Sonoma
P.O. Box 7456
San Francisco CA 94120-7456
Tel 800-541-2233
www.williams-sonoma.com
Excellent bakeware and tools, some ingredients. Available from mail order catalog or their many stores.

Crate & Barrel
Call (800) 967-6696 or visit www.crateandbarrel.com for retail outlet near you.
Stylish tableware and other items.

index

conversion charts

Weights and measures have been rounded up
or down slightly to make measuring easier.

volume equivalents

american	metric	imperial
1 teaspoon	5 ml	
1 tablespoon	15 ml	
¼ cup	60 ml	2 fl.oz.
⅓ cup	75 ml	2½ fl.oz.
½ cup	125 ml	4 fl.oz.
⅔ cup	150 ml	5 fl.oz. (¼ pint)
¾ cup	175 ml	6 fl.oz.
1 cup	250 ml	8 fl.oz.

weight equivalents: measurements:

imperial	metric	inches	cm
1 oz.	25 g	¼ inch	5 mm
2 oz.	50 g	½ inch	1 cm
3 oz.	75 g	¾ inch	1.5 cm
4 oz.	125 g	1 inch	2.5 cm
5 oz.	150 g	2 inches	5 cm
6 oz.	175 g	3 inches	7 cm
7 oz.	200 g	4 inches	10 cm
8 oz. (½ lb.)	250 g	5 inches	12 cm
9 oz.	275 g	6 inches	15 cm
10 oz.	300 g	7 inches	18 cm
11 oz.	325 g	8 inches	20 cm
12 oz.	375 g	9 inches	23 cm
13 oz.	400 g	10 inches	25 cm
14 oz.	425 g	11 inches	28 cm
15 oz.	475 g	12 inches	30 cm
16 oz. (1 lb.)	500 g		
2 lb.	1 kg		

oven temperatures:

225°F	110°C	Gas ¼
250°F	120°C	Gas ½
275°F	140°C	Gas 1
300°F	150°C	Gas 2
325°F	160°C	Gas 3
350°F	180°C	Gas 4
375°F	190°C	Gas 5
400°F	200°C	Gas 6
425°F	220°C	Gas 7
450°F	230°C	Gas 8
475°F	240°C	Gas 9